Farm House

A BUR OAK BOOK

Farm House

College Farm to University Museum

SECOND EDITION

Mary E. Atherly

Forewords by Gregory L. Geoffroy and Lynette L. Pohlman

Architectural history essay by Wesley Shank

UNIVERSITY OF IOWA PRESS / IOWA CITY

University of Iowa Press, Iowa City 52242
Copyright © 1995 by Iowa State University
Updated material copyright © 2009
by the University of Iowa Press
www.uiowapress.org
Printed in the United States of America

Royalties from the sale of this book are designated for
restoration of the Farm House.

The University of Iowa Press is a member of Green Press
Initiative and is committed to preserving natural resources.

Printed on acid-free paper

Library of Congress Cataloging-in-Publication Data
Atherly, Mary E.
    Farm House: college farm to university museum / by Mary E.
Atherly; forewords by Gregory L. Geoffroy and Lynette L.
Pohlman; architectural history essay by Wesley Shank.—2nd ed.
    p.   cm.
Includes index.
ISBN-13: 978-1-58729-810-3 (pbk.)
ISBN-10: 1-58729-810-4 (pbk.)
1. Iowa State University. Farm House Museum.   I. Shank,
Wesley I., 1927–.   II. Title.   III. Title: College farm to
university museum.
LD2547.A84 2009   2009000092
378.777'546—dc22

Contents

Foreword

Nestled in the northeast corner of the expansive and beautiful Iowa State University campus, the Farm House quietly and humbly represents the very essence of this great institution of higher learning and service.

More than one hundred and fifty years ago—on March 22, 1858—Iowa State University of Science and Technology was chartered as the Iowa Agricultural College and Model Farm. Before the agricultural college officially opened its doors in March 1869, there was a model farm, and the Farm House was its center. Built in 1860-1861 to house the model farm superintendent, the Farm House was the first permanent structure built on the campus. It stands today—beautifully restored—as a monument to the land-grant movement that reshaped higher education in our world and to the remarkable leadership of Iowa State University and the State of Iowa in shaping the mission of the land-grant universities.

The model farm carried out the first applied research in agriculture and farming practices and the Farm House became the bridge between this research and its practical application with Iowa farmers. This began several years before the passage of the Morrill Act in 1862 and Iowa's first-in-the-nation acceptance of the terms of the act. It shows how far ahead of the times Iowa was in creating egalitarian education. And with this head start, Iowa became agriculture's bellwether state and its land-grant institution the pioneer in defining the mission of these very special universities.

The Farm House also housed many of the university's prominent agricultural leaders. They included Seaman Knapp, James "Tama Jim" Wilson, and Charles Curtiss—people who literally shaped the development of modern agriculture in Iowa and the United States by spearheading such landmark national programs as extension and the experiment station research system.

With the publication of this second edition of *Farm House*, we are reminded of the continuing importance and relevance to today's world of the land-grant ideals of providing higher education access to all, combining practical education with the liberal arts and sciences, conducting applied research, and putting that research to work to improve peoples' lives. And every time we see and visit the Farm House Museum, we are reminded of the remarkable leadership role this university played in shaping the mission of these land-grant universities and of their tremendous impact on our world.

The Farm House Museum is an educational, historical, and cultural treasure. We are indebted to the many people whose vision, leadership, and generosity helped Iowa State preserve this very important part of our history. They made it possible for all who come to our campus to experience and learn about this wonderful history and rich tradition.

Gregory L. Geoffroy
President, Iowa State University

Director's Foreword

Iowa State University has seen significant changes throughout its history, and the Farm House has remained a constant presence through it all. Built on Iowa's prairie of waving grass, the Farm House was constructed in the early 1860s to establish the model farm for the new college. It became a home for the early families, faculty, and staff of the emerging college. These early residents gave birth to and then refined new ideas in higher education for the citizens of Iowa and later to the world. The Farm House is the prototype of the model farm, which has been followed for over a hundred and fifty years. Methods of agriculture and extension service were conceived and developed within the confines of the Farm House. Today it is a university museum where the ideals of education are still held in the highest esteem. As a museum the Farm House reveals the early history of Iowa State University and the people who lived and visited there.

This book includes the first significant research devoted to the people of the Farm House and to their social, cultural, and educational impact on the house itself and on Iowa State University. Mary Atherly, now-retired Farm House Museum curator, has spent years painstakingly researching sources in her efforts to discover the lifestyles of students, families, farmers, administrators, faculty, and guests who spent a portion of their lives in the Farm House. By offering insights into developing educational themes as the Farm House and Iowa State University moved through maturing stages from farm, to college, to university, this book goes beyond the architectural research that was compiled in the 1970s when structural restorations took place.

As Iowa State University continues its never-ending quest to be the best land-grant institution in the nation and a world educational leader, the Farm House and this book offer a reflection into our roots and traditions. Shortly before the printing of this second edition, we celebrated our university's 150th anniversary, when we remembered that the campus's founding structure was then—and remains—the Farm House. It reminds us that nineteenth-century leaders had a vision for the education of twentieth-century students, and that today, ISU leaders are carrying that vision into the twenty-first century. And it all began in the Farm House with people who pursued an educational vision on the prairie.

For this revised edition, I would like to thank Mary Atherly for her twenty-two years of professional service to the University Museums, and her nearly decade-long continued research efforts during her retirement years. Thanks to her, we now have an even more complete reflection of the early years at the Farm House.

Lynette L. Pohlman
Director and Chief Curator, University Museums
   Art on Campus Collection and Program
   Brunnier Art Museum
   Christian Petersen Art Museum
   Farm House Museum

Acknowledgments

The idea for a book about the history of the Farm House developed following a conversation in 1990 between Lynette Pohlman, director of the University Museums, and myself. She asked me what I would really like to do if I had all the time in the world. At that time, as curator of the Farm House Museum, I was most interested in researching the lives of the people who had lived at the Farm House. Little was actually known about them, except for brief information on the first and last residents. The mystery surrounding who they were and why they lived at the Farm House intrigued me. I wanted to tell the story in terms of what we knew rather than what we thought might have been. I believed the real story of the Farm House was not so much in the architectural significance of the house but in the people who had once lived and worked there.

The first edition of this book, printed in 1995, became a reality because of Bill Silag, then editor-in-chief at Iowa State University Press. He encouraged me to write the story of the Farm House so his "grandmother would enjoy reading it." I hope I have accomplished this.

The late Carl Hamilton graciously gave me his notes on the 1970s restoration of the Farm House. Debra Steilen organized these and several boxes of restoration documents and wrote the original draft of the first section of chapter 8. I was fortunate to witness the exterior restoration of the building in the 1990s and made daily notes about the process. Thank you to the museum staff for retaining these notes and photographs, which made it possible for me to write chapter 9.

A heartfelt thank you goes to the late Neva Petersen, who gave me my first tour of the Farm House and instilled in me her love for the house and for the people who make up this story. I would also like to thank Lynette Pohlman, who always encouraged me to do the impossible. Finally, I want to give a very special thank you to Sandra McJimsey, Dorothy Schwieder, and my husband, Alan, for their critical analyses, constructive criticism, and advice, all of which helped me shape this story.

Mary E. Atherly

Farm House

1 · *Tour of the Farm House Museum*

*O*nce a lonely structure on the prairie frontier, Iowa State University's Farm House stands among large, modern buildings in the midst of a busy campus. Stories and myths obscure the true history of the house but give rise to some interesting possibilities. One theory is that the Farm House really was an old stagecoach stop and tavern during the 1860s. Another story tells of secret tunnels in the basement where runaway slaves hid on their trip to freedom. A ghostly story shrouds a second-floor bedroom in mystery. Are these stories the true history of the house or is there more to be told?

The Farm House began in 1860 as a small, redbrick building in the middle of a prairie in Story County, Iowa. It was the first structure built on the land which is now the Iowa State University campus in Ames. Construction on the house began with volunteer labor and materials two years after the state legislature passed a measure providing for the establishment of a State Agricultural College and Model Farm. The house was intended to serve as the office and home for the farm manager and farmhands who would work on the college farm. Eventually, students who attended the college would work the farm as part of their practical experience in agriculture and report for their daily work assignments to the Farm House. As the college began to develop, the Farm House became its center. In the 1860s, it was the only finished house on the campus and was the first home to all the new faculty members, farm managers, farm superintendents and their families. Dr. Welch, the first college president, and his family spent their initial months at the college in the Farm House. He even wrote his 1869 inaugural speech in one of the upstairs bedrooms. The Farm House was where the Board of Trustees met and made crucial deci-

sions about the college. In the 1870s, shortly after the college officially opened its doors, the Farm House also served as the boarding
department and evening meals were often served to as many as 30
people, most of whom boarded at the house.

As the college grew in size and stature, the farm superintendent
position evolved into that of professor of agriculture and, eventually,
dean of agriculture. Seaman Knapp, the first professor of agriculture,
and his family lived in the house from 1880 to 1885, during which
time he became the second president of the college. When Knapp left
the college in 1886, the addition of two more rooms converted the
Farm House into a duplex. During the 1890s, renovations recreated a
comfortable single-family home for James "Tama Jim" Wilson, the first
director of the new agricultural experiment station at the college and
the first dean of agriculture. Charles F. Curtiss, the second dean of
agriculture, had moved his family into the Farm House in 1897,
where he lived for 50 years until his death in 1947. During this time,
the house became known as the "Curtiss House" and it is remembered by many today by that name. After Curtiss's death, three
women—Dr. Frances Carlin, Dr. Elizabeth Hoyt, and Beulah
McBride—rented the house until the fall of 1948, when it became a
home management house for one year. In the late summer of 1949,
the newly appointed dean of agriculture, Floyd Andre, and his family
moved into the Farm House. Andre would be the last dean of agriculture to live there. During his tenure, the house was declared a National Historic Landmark in 1965.

The house stood vacant after Dean Andre moved out in 1970
and was rescued from the demolition crews by a committee of dedicated volunteers whose vision and hard work directed the restoration
of the house. The committee decided to exhibit the house as it might
have looked during its first 50 years, 1860-1910, when the college was
just beginning to grow. Restored and furnished with donated 19th-
and early 20th-century furnishings, the Farm House was opened to
the public as a museum on July 4, 1976, the day the nation celebrated
its bicentennial.

Visitors to the university campus now reach the Farm House on
paved roads between well-kept grounds. Gone are the muddy, dirt
roads. A long, redbrick sidewalk now extends to the Farm House
front porch from the modern concrete walkway which was once a
gravel road. In the warmer months, flowers cascading from the boxes
on the porch railings give the house an inviting appearance. No mod-

ern doorbell announces visitors. A simple knock on the door brings a quick response and a friendly "Welcome to the Farm House" by museum staff or volunteers who frequently assist at the house. Once inside the Farm House, visitors often pause a minute in the main hallway adjusting to another time, another world.

Farm House, 1986, photographed from Ross Hall.
Courtesy of Iowa State University Library/University Archives

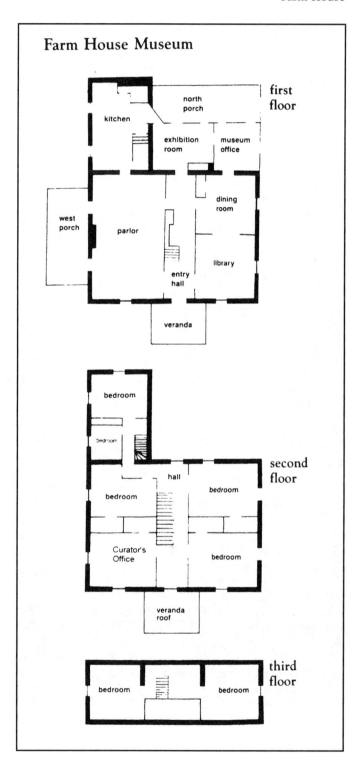

Floor plan of the Farm
House, 1994.
Farm House Museum Archives

The north side of the Farm House, 1994.
Photograph by Chuck Greiner, Front Porch Studio

   The impressive center hall of the main floor divides the house
evenly with two rooms on the right and a large room, once also two
rooms, on the left. A graceful walnut staircase along the west wall of
the hallway leads to the second floor. The entry and hallway with
their nine-foot ceilings are very inviting. Throughout the house, wallpaper reproduced from the late 19th-century era adds warmth to the
rooms. The front entry hall wallpaper with its pineapple design bids
a symbolic "welcome" to all that enter.
   To the left of the front hall is the formal parlor. The room now
looks as if it jumped out of a late 19th-century Victorian photograph
complete with oriental carpet, an Edison table phonograph, and lace
curtains at the window. This room actually began its life as two separate rooms. The front room served as the original office for the college farm. The back room was a sitting room for the boarders. Orig-

Main hallway on the first floor and the staircase to the second floor.
Photograph by Chuck Greiner, Front Porch Studio

inally there was a door on the west wall where farmhands could enter directly from the yard without leaving mud tracks all over the house. That door is no longer there and a large French door is now in its place. During the Farm House's first 30 years, large potbellied stoves heated these rooms but were replaced with radiators connected to a central furnace in 1896. Two of the original radiators, which have been painted over many times, still keep the parlor warm during the coldest weather.

We are not certain exactly who removed the wall between these two rooms. It may have been James "Tama Jim" Wilson in the 1890s to provide the Wilsons with a formal parlor for his daughter Flora's famous musicals. However, we do know the most dramatic changes to the room occurred about 1910-12. At that time, workers from the college laid golden oak floors over the original plank floors. They also added a fireplace. Tall glass French doors replaced the windows on either side of the new fireplace. These doors led out onto a newly constructed screened porch.

College alumni and friends of the Farm House Museum's renovation project donated all the furnishings in the house including the 1890s parlor furniture. Unfortunately, very few items actually used by people living in the Farm House have found their way back to the house. The exceptions in the parlor are a black and white 19th-cen-

West parlor on the first floor, looking south. The oriental carpet is from the Curtiss family and the large upholstered chair is from the Knapp family.
Photograph by Chuck Greiner, Front Porch Studio

tury engraving, an oriental rug from the Curtiss family, and a large red plush chair once owned by Seaman Knapp.

The parlor often appears dark and mysterious with only one long window at the south end. The only other light comes through the two glass French doors on the west. Mornings in the room are shaded from the sun, which makes it cool in the summer but cold and dark in the winter.

At the back of the room the doorway leads directly into what was the 1860s kitchen. As you walk through the doorway you walk into yet another time period. The floors are wide plank boards cut from timber grown on the college farm. The bright white walls are a result of a "white wash" paint formulated from a 19th-century recipe. A walnut wainscoting goes around the entire room. Fourteen layers of paint were removed from the wainscoting during renovation in the 1970s to expose the beautiful wood beneath.

The room has an astounding six doors leading to other areas of the house. The only interior stairway to the basement is through one of these six doors. Another door leads to a very narrow, curved stairway to the second floor. Yet another door, when opened, reveals a brick wall. This doorway once led to the washroom attached to the kitchen, but it was later bricked over when the washroom was torn down in the 1890s. The room then became a bedroom. The bricks are of interest because they were found in the basement and were left over from the construction of the house in the 1860s. Looking at these red bricks, you can see how soft and irregular the handmade bricks on the exterior of the house really are. Stucco now covers the red bricks on the exterior of the house to prevent their further deterioration.

The kitchen is furnished to reflect the early days of its use before water was piped into the house. The furnishings are simple: a pie safe for the storage of cooked foods, a table for preparing and eating meals, a dry sink, water bucket, a braided rag rug, and a small coal burning stove. Above the dry sink, an antique rifle hangs ready to shoot some prairie chickens for dinner.

Although this room is called the kitchen it is also referred to as a "dining room" in the *College Farm Journal* of the 1860s. It brings up a puzzling question. Was this room really a cooking kitchen or was the cooking done in the attached wood washroom? There is no evidence that a wall hole for a stovepipe ever existed. Nor is there any chimney extending from this room. Maybe we will never know for certain.

The doorway on the east wall once led directly to the outside.

West original kitchen, looking south.
Photograph by Chuck Greiner, Front Porch Studio

It now leads into a back entry room with a lower ceiling. This room and the adjacent room to the east are believed to have been added to the house in 1886 to create a duplex by adding a second kitchen to the house. These are the only rooms in the house without a full basement; they rest on a foundation only three bricks deep. The bricks have shifted over the years and the back door is a wonderful study in leaning doorways. When the door frame dropped on one side, someone just cut off wood at the top of the door to accommodate that drop, giving the entire doorway a most curious appearance. The chimney in this room may have been used for the kitchen that was added in 1886 and the furnace that was installed in 1896. An excavation under the rooms in 1991 revealed evidence of a fire in the floor, possibly from a stove. After 1900, this room was a laundry room. Rumors remain about Dean Curtiss using this room to take his bath in a large metal bathtub. It was, after all, next to the kitchen and, more importantly, hot water.

The room to the east, the kitchen of the 1900s, now serves the museum as a preparation room for events. It can be the coldest or the hottest room in the house. The last resident of the house, Dean Floyd Andre, said that even with the radiators on full, the temperature in the kitchen often plunged to near freezing during the winter.

As you walk through the doorway from the back entry room into the main hallway, you pass through what was an original back door to the house. Before 1886 and the addition of the two frame rooms, you could step out this back door onto a brick courtyard of the then U-shaped house. A few steps into the hallway toward the front of the hall, an abandoned trap door and stairway to the cellar is now covered with oak flooring.

Dining room.
Photograph by Chuck Greiner, Front Porch Studio

To the left of the back hallway is the current dining room. It wasn't always the dining room. Before the 1886 addition of a second kitchen, this room was the farm office and secretary's office. Later in the 1880s when the house was a duplex, it was the living quarters for the farm superintendent. It became a dining room in the late 1890s.

On sunny days, the room is bright with light shining through the lace curtains in the one tall window in the room. On dark, gloomy days, the center chandelier creates a pleasant warm glow in the room. As people enter the room, the wallpaper causes the most comment. The busy, bold overall pattern of fruit-laden baskets is typical of a late 19th-century home but may be somewhat foreign to modern decorating tastes. Although no remnants or records remain of the actual wallpaper used before the 1900s, this pattern was used in homes in the early 20th century. The wallpaper also covers the radiator pipes leading to the second floor to prevent unsightly pipes from intruding into the family's dining experience.

An ornate, large round table and chairs fill the center of the room. Mrs. Olive Curtiss lived in the Farm House from 1897 until her death in 1943 and gave frequent luncheons in this room. Olive set an elegant table but maintained a simple centerpiece by using her best crystal bowls. Two of those bowls now belong to the Farm House Museum. The large china cabinet with its rounded glass doors holds Haviland china once used by members of the Curtiss family. A simple walnut sideboard holds more china and crystal on display for special occasions. Often displayed above the sideboard is a watercolor painting of lilacs done in 1901 by Etta May Budd, who lived in the Farm House with her family in 1877. Miss Budd later taught art at Simpson College, where she met George Washington Carver. It was she who encouraged Carver to pursue a college career at Iowa State College.

The large archway in the dining room opens directly into the library. What appears to be missing from the room are sliding doors that might have separated it from the library. However, a former student who lived in the house in 1936 said that, even then, the rooms were open to each other.

The only existing photograph of the interior of the house prior to 1910 shows this library as used by Dean Charles Curtiss in 1907. The *Iowa Agriculturalist* magazine of 1907 featured that photograph with an article explaining the merits of a well thought-out decorating plan for a pleasant and inviting room. The photograph is being used as a guide to reconstructing this room. Unfortunately, the article did

Southeast library on the first floor.
Photograph by Chuck Greiner, Front Porch Studio

not mention a most important ingredient—color.

Friends of the University Museums have been successful in obtaining an antique ceiling lighting fixture and the return of the black carved wood armchair. Not pictured in the 1907 photograph but once belonging to Dean Curtiss is the small Roycroft bookcase. This triangular bookcase, presented to Curtiss by the class of 1901, bears the inscription "1901 CFC." The library also now contains other artifacts which reflect late Victorian values and views of the world.

A fireplace in the east corner of the library warmed the room from its construction around 1910 through the late 1940s when it was removed. The fireplace was reconstructed in 2006 after the discovery of the original firebox. As you leave this room and again enter the main hallway, you can see from the door frame that a door originally closed this room off from the hall.

The stairway to the second floor is made of walnut and the banister still gleams after 130 years of use. Of course, the steps and rail-

Second-floor landing, with a portrait of Charles F. Curtiss on the left and an International Livestock trophy on the corner table.
Photograph by Chuck Greiner, Front Porch Studio

ing received a sanding and polishing during the renovation of the 1970s. Still it is amazing how solid and beautiful the stairway remains. There are 14 stairs in the staircase. It is a steep climb, forcing most people to hold on to the banister on their way to the second floor. Imagine climbing these stairs wearing the clothing of the 1860s when women's long skirts would drag on the steps.

At the top of the landing you can see down the length of the hall leading to some of the six bedrooms on this floor. The bedrooms on the left of the stairway are shielded from view. On the north wall hangs an antique telephone. The college phone system, which began before the local Ames phone system, at first reached only the college buildings and offices. Dean Curtiss was a practical man and preferred his phone on the second floor near his bedroom. His daughter once said that the only calls he received were at night, usually about a problem at one of the college farm buildings.

Around the corner and to the left of the landing is the bedroom once said to be used for storing seeds in the 1860s. This room began as two smaller rooms. The transom above the one door locates the entry to the smaller of the two original rooms. It had a false dropped ceiling and no window. The room adjacent to it was lit with a large west window and had a large closet. This two-room arrangement did not last very long. The dropped ceiling and wall separating the rooms were removed in the late 1860s to create one L-shaped room. It became a most prized bedroom because of the cross ventilation provided by the two doors and the transom. From this room, you can step through the window onto the roof of the west screened porch. In the 1950s this was Jacqueline Andre's room, and the Andre children used this window to escape for afternoon sun bathing on the

L-shaped bedroom left of the landing and a view of the hallway on the second floor.
Photograph by Chuck Greiner, Front Porch Studio

Hallway and staircase in the second-floor west kitchen ell.
Photograph by Chuck Greiner, Front Porch Studio

porch roof. The room is now filled with furnishings typical of the early 1900s.

To reach the north bedrooms, you cross from the main hall outside the L-shaped bedroom and through a doorway that was once an exterior wall. A step down into the back hall shows that the front main house and the original small kitchen wing did not meet when opened to each other. It's possible the kitchen wing was not intended to open into the main portion of the house, so this might not have been a concern at the time.

As you enter this area of the house, the ceilings are 18 inches lower than the nine-foot ceilings in the main portion of the house. These lower ceilings also slope on either side. Immediately visible on the right is the narrow, winding stairway to the first floor. The stairway is structurally sound but is no longer used because of its small steps and steep, twisting turns.

Off this short back hall are two small bedrooms. No one knows for certain if these were originally two bedrooms or if the smaller room was walled off from the hall at a later date. Typically, the upstairs of farm homes were open and the children slept in a dormitory style although the parents may have had a separate room.

On the ceiling above the stairway you can see a faint outline of a skylight. In 1867, A. J. Graves, the first farm manager, installed a skylight for ventilation over this stairway and another one in the north bedroom at the end of the short hall. The skylights remained in the rooms until the 1970s renovation when they were removed during a reroofing project. Someday reinstallation of skylights will return the rooms to their former appearance.

The first residents of the Farm House, the Fitchpatrick family, moved into the house in 1861 when the main portion of the house was just a shell. The only finished rooms were the kitchen and the two rooms above it. These rooms are small by any measure. Imagine

Southwest bedroom in the second-floor kitchen ell, 2007.
Photograph by Bob Elbert, Courtesy of Iowa State University

the Fitchpatrick family with eight children living in this space. Then also imagine boarding the local schoolteacher for most of the year. It must have been very cozy to say the least.

The smaller of the two rooms is now used as a bedroom and sewing room. Before the 20th century, most clothing was made at home. Often a seamstress would come and spend a week or so sewing for the family. We know the Curtiss girls, who grew up in the house in the early 1900s, enjoyed creating their own dresses and used this area for sewing.

The larger of the two rooms is at the center of a ghost story invented, admittedly, by Neva Petersen, a prominent member of the Farm House restoration committee. Apparently, the white gauze curtains on the window of the north wall would not stay where they were put. Each time the house was entered for a tour, the curtains appeared to be moved aside as if someone had been looking out the window. To explain this, Neva said she thought it was the ghost of

North bedroom in the second-floor kitchen ell, 2007.
Photograph by Bob Elbert, Courtesy of Iowa State University

Ruth Curtiss looking out the window for her boyfriend as he approached the Farm House. Although later it was found to be the janitor who just happened to like looking out the window, the story seems to prevail and has spooked many a new employee of the museum.

The room certainly doesn't look as if it should be the center of a ghost story. The double bed, desk, rocking horse, and homespun curtains give the room a warm, friendly feeling. The outline of the skylight on the east sloped ceiling is still visible. This was Richard Andre's bedroom when he lived in the house in the 1950s and 60s, and he has fond memories of lying in bed at night looking at the sky and stars through the skylight.

Back in the main hallway, across from the staircase to the east, are two bedrooms with large closets that back up to each other. Each closet has more than one lock; this was important to people who rented rooms in the house and wanted security for their valuables. These two bedrooms have enough room for more than one bed and

Northeast bedroom on the second floor.
Photograph by Chuck Greiner, Front Porch Studio

South end of the second-floor hallway, the location of the ca. 1896 bathroom. *Photograph by Chuck Greiner, Front Porch Studio*

they probably had more than one when the house was used for boarders.

The northeast bedroom combines late 19th-century machine-made furniture with hand-crafted objects. This could be the master bedroom.

A large washbasin and pitcher are prominent on the dressing table, as is the ceramic chamber pot under the bed. Fortunately for those who lived in the Farm House before the advent of indoor toilets, a large 10-foot-square brick privy was just a short walk behind the house. Still, a chamber pot under the bed was welcome, especially during cold winter nights.

Southeast bedroom on the second floor.
Photograph by Chuck Greiner, Front Porch Studio

Kerosene lamps provided light in the room before the days of electrical lights. During the day, sun streaming through the two windows provided sufficient light to read or sew. A small, black, coal stove connects to one of the five chimneys on the outside wall of the house. This same type of stove would have provided the room with excellent heat during the coldest weather. The rag rug on the floor and the handmade quilt on the bed all add to the charm of this room and give it a very comfortable, homey feel.

The alcove at the south end of the second-floor hallway is now used as a sitting area, a familiar sight in homes in the late 19th century. Oddly enough, this was the location of one of the first "water closets" built into the house in 1896. Prior to that time, it may have been used as a closet or storage room. Walls were removed during the renovation project in the 1970s to open the area and give added light to the hallway.

The southeast bedroom is perhaps the brightest room in the house. Even on gloomy days, the room appears to be wrapped in light. Any Victorian would enjoy using this room. The 19th-century-style strawberry wallpaper is bright and cheery. A marble-topped dresser and a dark wood chest of drawers are typical of the late 1890s when bedrooms were also used as sitting rooms where adults could have private time to read or perhaps write a letter to a friend.

Across the hallway to the west is the sixth bedroom on this floor. This room suffered structural damage in the 1960s when the floor support beam cracked. At one point, the wall pulled away from the floor a full inch. A new steel floor support beam relieved the problem but the walls still don't meet the floor. The room is not open to the public and is used as a museum curator's office and storage area. Few people are aware that this room even exists because it is

Hallway and landing on the third floor, looking east.
Photograph by Chuck Greiner, Front Porch Studio

hidden when the adjacent door to the third-floor stairway is opened against it.

The stairway to the third floor is even steeper than the kitchen stairway. Visitors are cautioned, "Watch your head!" when they reach the landing. At this point, the ceiling slopes to four feet and many heads have hit the ceiling wondering what happened. The railings at the top of the stairs assist visitors and provide a measure of safety. The landing originally was open to the stairs without a rail. Early records of the Farm House indicate these rooms were rented to farmhands and domestic workers in the house. You can almost see the men (women wore long skirts that made it difficult to do anything except walk down the steps) jumping from the side landing onto the stairs as they hurried to get the morning fires started or rushed off to do their farm chores.

There are two bedrooms on this floor, one on either side of the center hall. The sloped ceilings on both sides of each room make the placement of furniture a challenge. The rooms have large closets, and

West bedroom on the third floor.
Photograph by Chuck Greiner, Front Porch Studio

East bedroom on the third floor, 2007.
Photograph by Bob Elbert, Courtesy of Iowa State University

there are even larger closets under the eaves. The floors are the original wide plank boards and frequently squeak if you step in the right (or wrong) place. Each room has one window that faces out across the lawn and campus. It must have been a spectacular view across the farm fields and open lawns before the large classroom buildings encroached on the Farm House.

These rooms have seen many changes and uses over the years. First used as bedrooms, they also were used as children's playrooms, storage space, and finally a workshop. Dean Andre, an avid woodworker, brought his power saw to the third floor and used the west bedroom as a workshop. He must have blown numerous fuses because the entire third floor has only four electrical outlets, two in each room. Today, the third-floor bedrooms are furnished in a simpler style more typical of rooms used by boarders. Large traveling trunks hold the personal possessions of the imaginary renters. The rooms have a cozy, homey feeling.

No tour of the house would be complete without a peep into the basement, which is the scene for one of the most interesting myths about the house. Only two of the original stairways to the basement remain. The basement was built in two stages, the smaller room under the original kitchen and then the larger basement under the main portion of the house. At least four entrances to the basement once existed: two outside entrances on the east and west sides of the house, and two inside stairways, one from the kitchen and the other through a trap door in the main hallway. The two remaining entrances to the basement are via the original kitchen stairway and an east outside entrance. Remnants of the hallway staircase are still visible in the basement.

The basement was built to be used for storing farm produce but later proved to be too damp. The original brick floor can now be seen but was once so covered with dirt no one realized it was there. The entire basement now looks like a forest of steel trees with support beams and metal jack posts placed there during the 1970s, and again

North foundation wall in the cellar, with the opening to the crawl space beneath the east kitchen, ca. 1970.
Farm House Museum Archives.

in the 1990s to support the floors. The basement walls are thick gray stone and you can see where windows and doorways once existed. You can also see where portions of the wall are gone, which brings us to the myth about the Farm House being a station on the underground railroad during the 1860s.

In 1896, James "Tama Jim" Wilson installed a furnace in the basement and connected the house to a system of radiators. In order to pipe heat into the two wooden rooms added in 1886, a large hole was made in the north wall of the basement to give access to the area under the two rooms. To the casual eye, the area under these rooms looked as if the dirt floor could indeed be a tunnel to mysterious places and, more importantly, a wonderful hiding place. As time dimmed memories of the original reason for the hole in the wall, gradually the question of why it was there raised the possibility that it was a hiding place for runaway slaves during the Civil War. It seemed reasonable since Iowa was a free state and there was an active underground railroad network here. But since the area under the back rooms where the slaves purportedly were hidden did not even exist until 1886, it seems unlikely that slaves hid there. It also seems unlikely that the Farm House was involved in the underground network this far north of the historically accepted route. Yet, who knows?

Visitors to the Farm House are often astounded by the size of the house. When the house was first built it stood alone on the prairie. Now it is dwarfed by large classroom buildings. Visitors also mention that the house is hard to find. We like to tell them that the Farm House was here first and every other building came later. The Farm House continues to charm and fascinate visitors. It is and always will be a unique part of the history of the university. It is a history of people with vision who struggled with a "farmers' college and farm" and influenced the development of the college into an internationally recognized university.

2 · *Origin and Construction of the Farm House*

*I*n a lecture entitled *Iowa, A Character Study,* Tom Morain, former director of education at the Des Moines Living History Farms, describes Iowans as having a unique sense of "US-ness" about them. It comes, he says, from a background of strong family partnerships, family farms, and small rural communities. This same sense of family partnerships combined with a strong work ethic existed in the early settlers of Iowa who began streaming into the Iowa territory just after it opened for settlement in 1833. They brought with them their hopes for a better life for their children. Many of these families gave up the comforts of settled homes to begin again on the prairie. This same spirit of determination, this "US-ness," brought people together in Story and Boone counties and helped them build a college on the wind-swept prairie.

John B. Newhall, in 1846, was the first to record the sites of these families headed for the Iowa prairie and rich virgin farmlands. He wrote, "The roads would be literally lined with the long blue wagons of the emigrants slowly wending their way over the broad prairies—the cattle and hogs, men and dogs, and frequently women and children, forming the rear of the van—often ten, twenty, and thirty wagons in company."

By 1838, just five years after the first wagon trains crossed into the Iowa territory, 23,000 people called Iowa home. These people were a marked contrast to the early explorers and trappers who only passed through the territory. They were here to build homes, to start farms, and to raise their families. They came from farms in Germany, Great Britain, Holland, and the Scandinavian countries. Even the doctors, lawyers, ministers, and teachers among the early settlers made their living by farming.

The eastern edge of Iowa developed very quickly. It took just until 1846, 13 years after the first settlers crossed into Iowa, for it to

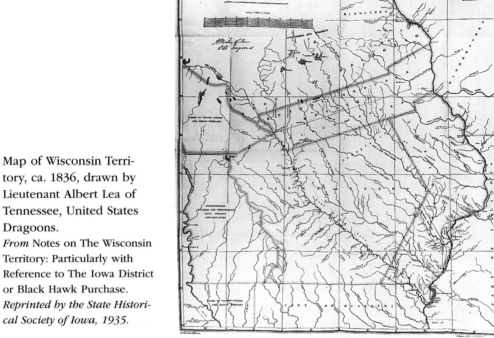

Map of Wisconsin Terri-
tory, ca. 1836, drawn by
Lieutenant Albert Lea of
Tennessee, United States
Dragoons.
From Notes on The Wisconsin
Territory: Particularly with
Reference to The Iowa District
or Black Hawk Purchase.
*Reprinted by the State Histori-
cal Society of Iowa, 1935.*

become a state. Iowa City, 90 miles west of the Illinois border, became the first state capital and the location of the State University of
Iowa, which would be chartered in 1847.

Streams and rivers crisscrossed the prairie in the center of the
new state creating areas of dense marsh and swamplands. Around
these areas were some of the best black soils in the state. Story
County, incorporated in the mid-1850s, encompassed lands cut by the
Skunk River on the east and Squaw Creek on the west. The county
was sparsely populated, only a few log cabins dotted the landscape.
Boone County, adjacent to Story County on the west, grew at a faster
rate. By 1852, there were 1,000 people living in Boone County and
only 214 in Story County.

The families that came to Iowa had definite ideas about their fu-
tures. They wanted many of the same things we want today: jobs, education, and a better life for their children—and there were lots of
children. (In 1860 one-third of Iowa's population was under the age

of 10.) Education was a high priority but not the classical education usually available only to the rich. They wanted education that would teach their children modern farming methods. The new, more complicated farm implements and technical advancements required a specialized education that most farm parents could not provide their children. These families also wanted an education for their children that they could afford.

One solution for an affordable education was proposed by Suel Foster of Muscatine, Iowa, in 1847. The state agricultural school system in Germany greatly impressed Foster. In the German system, students spent part of their day working on a farm, which paid for their tuition, and part of their day in classes. He thought this system offered just what Iowa needed—a practical education for the benefit of farm families. Foster knew that he would be up against strong oppo-

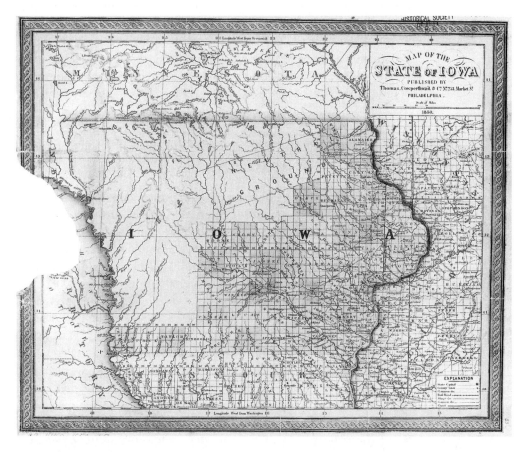

State of Iowa, 1850.
State Historical Society of Iowa

sition to establishing yet another state-supported college in Iowa. Beginning in 1838, the territory and later the state of Iowa chartered 58 colleges only to see most of them fail for lack of financial support. The State University of Iowa in Iowa City received its charter the same year Foster proposed starting an agricultural college. Foster believed that the classical education that was to be provided at the State University of Iowa would not serve the growing number of farm families seeking an agricultural education for their children. Although Foster wrote to the leading farmers in the state seeking support for the college, his idea gained little recognition until 1858.

Three young Iowa legislators headed by Benjamin Gue, a future trustee of the proposed college, drafted a bill on February 4, 1858, for an agricultural college. Support for the agricultural college came from members of the State Agriculture Society. The state legislature did not agree. How, they asked, could Iowa support another state college and why couldn't the agricultural interests be satisfied with courses at the State University in Iowa City? To many it simply didn't make financial sense. Proponents argued that the idea of a practical farmers' college was not compatible with the classical philosophy of teaching at the State University. Gue and his fellow supporters of the agricultural college nearly lost the fight. Finally, after a narrow vote of 25 in favor and 24 against, the bill passed. On March 22, 1858, Governor Lowe signed the bill into law and established a "State Agricultural College and Model Farm to be connected with the entire Agricultural Interests of the State."

The state of Iowa now had an agricultural college—at least on paper. As soon as the governor appointed the Board of Trustees it was up to them to find land for the college and farm, build the college buildings, select a faculty, and finance all the expenses connected with the college. Toward this ambitious undertaking, the state of Iowa gave the trustees a total of $10,000 and their good wishes.

Suel Foster took charge of the newly established college as president of the Board of Trustees. The other members of the board were J. W. Henderson, E. G. Day, Timothy Day, John Wright, G. W. F. Sherwin, William Duane Wilson, John Pattee, Richard Gaines, Peter Melendy, and Moses W. Robinson. Melendy and Robinson would later serve as superintendents of the college farm. All of the men were leading members of the agricultural community in the state.

The Board of Trustees was eager to hire a faculty and select a site for the college. E. G. Day, a trustee from Story County, began a campaign to bring the college to his county. To some, however, Story County seemed the last place for a college.

Day found local support for the college among the farmers in both Story and Boone counties. Washington T. Graham, an early settler in Story County, shared Day's enthusiasm for the new college. Graham, however, may have been more interested in selling his land to the college than in having the college as a neighbor. Graham purchased his farm, located southwest of Squaw Creek in western Story County, in the early 1850s. He was already making plans to sell some of the land to the railroads when the agricultural college became a possibility.

Graham's new neighbor to the northwest, Louis Badger, owned approximately 130 acres of prairie with a mature grove of walnut and oak trees on its northern edge. Badger and his father bought the Iowa land, sight unseen, while living in Indiana during the spring of 1858. Just about everything Badger knew about Iowa came from the newspapers that he read religiously. Although Louis Badger was totally unaware of Graham's

Benjamin Gue.
Courtesy of Iowa State University Library/University Archives

H. L. Badger (*center*) and friends, ca. 1860.
Courtesy of Charles M. Conger

plans for the college, it probably wouldn't have changed his mind about coming to Iowa if he had known. After all it was Graham who wanted to sell his land to the state, not Louis Badger. While Graham and Day were out gathering support to locate the new agricultural college in Story County, Louis Badger prepared his family for the journey to Iowa.

On a hot August day in 1858, Louis Badger, his wife, Mary, and infant son, and Dwight Badger, Louis's brother, boarded a train in Indiana headed for Iowa. All their family possessions were aboard the train—boxes of household goods, tools for the new farm and their horses. They arrived in Iowa City on September 1, 1858. They made the rest of the journey by wagon and horseback. The Badger family rented a cabin from Washington T. Graham, who probably told them about the possibility of a college being built in the county. It did not seem to affect Badger's plans for his farm.

Badger kept a handwritten diary of his family's trip across the Iowa prairie to their new home. He paints a vivid picture of the struggles faced by a typical family setting up a home and farm in Story County in 1858. Badger made almost daily entries in his diary during the fall of 1858. Three entries in the diary talk about his new home:

> *September 17.* Got our house in Sleepy Hollow cleared out and our other load from Nevada stowed over in it and after a supper of Prairie chicken without salt, we went to bed.
> *September 27.* Hewed lumber for house. Killed a squirrel for breakfast, almost sick in forenoon…
> *October 13.* Went to mill to get another load of lumber and jars from Fitchpatricks (in New Philadelphia).…Filled bed ticking with straw, helped salt meat, cut firewood for supper and turned out cattle.

In 1858, New Philadelphia was a thriving community on the western edge of the county. William Fitchpatrick, the future first resident of the Farm House, operated a hardware store there and owned a large tract of farmland east of Graham's. Badger made the five-mile trip to New Philadelphia several times a week to purchase supplies and the county newspaper and to collect his mail.

The one local paper, the *Story County Advocate,* carried an article on November 17, 1858, about the competition for the location of a new agricultural college. The article also encouraged attendance at a meeting on November 27 "to rally behind the college cause." E. G. Day followed up on this article with one of his own on November 30,

1858. He asked local residents to send him samples of seeds, grasses, minerals, and stones in Story County that he hoped would convince the college trustees that Story County was the ideal place for the agricultural college. The *Advocate* carried other notices on December 8 and 15 setting Christmas Day, December 25, 1858, for a community meeting for the sole purpose of generating support for the agricultural college.

It is difficult to imagine Iowans today taking seriously a public meeting called on Christmas Day. It was quite different on that Christmas Day Saturday in 1858. The Story County Courthouse in Nevada was alive with excitement. People came from Boone County, 15 miles to the west, from New Philadelphia, from Cambridge to the south, from Nevada, and from farms throughout Story County. They made the arduous trip across frozen mud roads and partially frozen streams to take part in the meeting that would determine the fate of the "farmers' college."

The gavel sounded the beginning of the meeting. George Maxwell accepted the role as chair and quickly appointed 10 men, one from each of the townships in the county, to a committee to help write any resolutions proposed during the meeting. Washington T. Graham represented Washington Township and led the discussion. The committee's first attempt at a resolution met with a loud protest. They proposed giving 12,000 acres of swampland in the county or the proceeds from its sale to the college. No one at the meeting believed for a minute that offering swampland would be an incentive to the college trustees to locate the new college in Story County, and the committee was sent back to their pens and paper. The final version deleted any reference to swampland and instead pledged $10,000 in county bonds for the college. The next step would be to persuade all the voters in the county to back this proposal.

We know Graham attended the meeting, and it is likely Badger did too. The first reference to the college in Badger's diary appears on December 28, 1858, three days after the meeting. He wrote, "Graham is anxious to sell his farm for a State Farm." Badger did not include any comments on how he felt about the state farm.

The organizers of the Christmas Day meeting held other public meetings throughout the county during January to explain the proposal and to generate support for the college. Election day was February 7, 1859. The proposal—selling $10,000 in county bonds to support the college—passed by a large majority. In addition to the sale of the bonds, the people in Story and Boone counties pledged another $5,500 in cash and more than 1,000 acres of good farmland scattered throughout the counties to be used for the benefit of the college. W. G. Allen from Story County headed the delegation appointed to make the presentation to the college Board of Trustees.

Story County wasn't the only county interested in the new college. The trustees received similar proposals from Marshall, Polk, Johnson, and Kossuth counties. Each county sent samples of grasses, seeds, and soil to the trustees for their inspection. Trustees Sherwin, Pattee, and Gaines made up the committee that inspected the sites proposed for the college. Louis Badger recorded their visits in his diary for 1859:

> *June 8.* Ploughing, harrowing and marking out corn
> ground....Commissioners here to look at land for
> Model farm.
> *June 13.* Commissioners up and took a look at land
> again.

The trustees made their final decision on June 21, 1859, after numerous votes. Story County was the winner. The offer of land, money, and labor to build the college made the difference. Some of the people from Story County who offered money weren't quite certain where they would get it, but they did their best to provide assistance in building the college.

The decision to purchase land in Story County for the college was not without opposition. One state legislator remarked:

> Since the board [of Trustees] has made the location
> for the farm and college where they have it, it would
> be well for them to locate a cemetery on the farm so
> as to be ready to bury the dead; for there will be a
> demand for one at such an unhealthy location....I un-
> derstand it to be but little short of a frog pond.

This legislator's opinion didn't matter to Story or Boone county farmers. They had the college, and it was up to them to prove the location was the right one. To celebrate their success, they held a countywide picnic on July 4, 1859. They chose to celebrate this event on the site of the new college farm. They selected a cool spot under a grove of trees located on the edge of the property. This grove of trees was the northwest corner of Louis Badger's land. Today this area is north of Pammel Drive, between the Communications Building and the college cemetery.

The celebration that took place on the college farm that Fourth of July was a community event with speeches and toasts honoring everyone who helped win the college for Story County. W. G. Allen later noted the extraordinary meal provided by the women. They set two long tables under the trees for the food. Those attending, he wrote, "ate a feast of peas, potatoes, fruit, pies, beets, cheese, honey, ham, mutton, fish, turkey, chicken, roast pig and other delicacies and substantials." Louis Badger noted the event in his diary: "Monday, July 4 [1859]. Went fishing. Simmons here in morning. Celebration in grove."

Four families sold land to the state to make up the original college and farm. (Later records list five families involved in the original sale but the official country records list only four. The college did acquire an additional 10 acres on the northwest edge of the original farm but the records on this section are confusing, listing a purchase in the 1860s then resale and later a final sale to the college in 1932.) Louis (Lewis) and Lucy Badger of Ohio deeded 129.96 acres to the state for $1,100 on July 6, 1859. Henry McCarthy of Story County sold his "200 and 40 acres more or less" on July 16, 1859, for $1,549.36, which was less than its actual value, as part of his contribution to the college. Absalom and Deborah Cooper of Lawrence County, Indiana, sold their 228.04 acres for $2,280.40 and Samuel and Davey Luther of Boone County sold the final "40 some" acres to the state on June 28, 1859, for $449.96. The official description of the land includes the western half of Section 3 and three-quarters of Section 4, Range 24W of Washington Township. The total spent for the land was $5,379.72, which came from the original $10,000 given to the Board of Trustees by the state.

Washington T. Graham was deeply disappointed that his land was not included in the sale to the state. A true entrepreneur at heart, he later drew up a proposal for his land, called "College Town," which W. G. Allen surveyed in 1863. When the town didn't happen, he offered a portion of his land to the railroad for a station if they would just run their tracks through his property. This didn't happen either. The railroad eventually laid tracks through the college farm to the north. In 1864, the town of Ames developed along the train tracks east of the college farm.

County Surveyor R. H. Mitchell completed the first official survey of the college farm on September 3, 1859, at the request of Trustee Day. Since it was late in the growing season, the trustees

Record of the 1859 sale of Badger's land to state of Iowa for the college farm.
Courtesy of Story County Recorder's Office, Nevada, Iowa

waited until the following spring to start work on the farm. Their first priority for the college farm was a barn and a farmer's house. It was essential to establish a recognizable college farm on the prairie to put an end to any doubts about the college's existence. The Board of Trustees appointed board member Richard Gaines as agent for the farm with the responsibility for getting the project started.

In 1859 some of the land was ready for planting on Badger's section of the farm. As part of the sale of his land, Badger also agreed to have additional land broken and plowed the following year. Getting the thick black soil ready for planting was slow, backbreaking work. Teams of six or eight oxen pulled the sod-breaking plows. Once the steel plows turned over the sod, the farmers chopped the thick black chunks of soil with axes to further break them up before planting could begin.

Trustees Suel Foster, Daniel McCarthy, and E. G. Day met on the college farm early in 1860 to select the site for the farmer's house and barns. They chose a site for the house near the center of the farm, on high ground, in a field of tall prairie grass. They marked the site using a compass and surveyor's chain, and McCarthy drove in the first stake. They decided to build the barns northeast of the house. There wasn't any money for a college building, so that site decision was left to much later.

There seems to be genuine confusion about the actual design for the farmer's house. Milens Burt presented a plan to the trustees but no record exists today of his vision of a farmer's house. It is commonly believed that the house took shape as it was built. Gaines enlisted the help of those who earlier pledged their support of money and labor to get the farm started. Actual work began on the house and barn during the spring of 1860. Donated labor and hard work went into these buildings. People took time away from their own

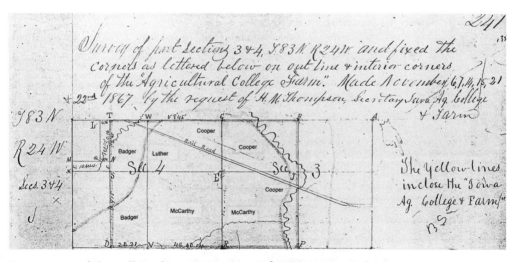

Survey map of the college farm, November 1867. (The names of owners who sold land to the state were added to the map by the author.)
Courtesy of Story County Recorder's Office, Nevada, Iowa

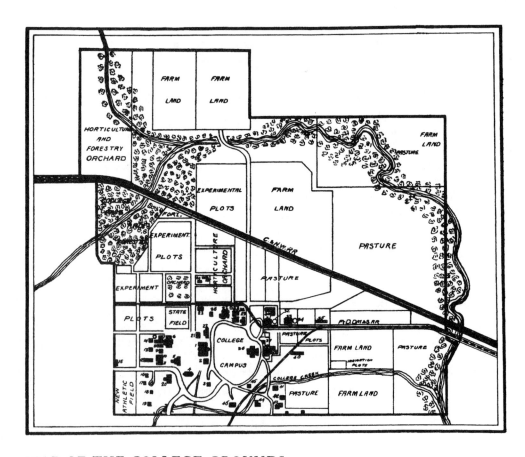

MAP OF THE COLLEGE GROUNDS

1 Central Building
2 Superintendent of Buildings, Office
3 Residence of Dean Stanton
4 Alumni Hall
5 Chemical Hall
6 Engineering Hall
7 Engineering Annex
8 Pattern Shop
9 Foundry
10 Power House
11 Hydraulic Laboratory
12 Machine Shop
13 Forge Shop
14 Training Shed
15 West Gate Station
16 Residence of Professor Holden

17 Residence of Professor Beyer
18 Residence of Dean Marston
19 Residence
20 College Hospital
21 Post Office and Bookstore
22 Morrill Hall
23 Central Station
24 Residence of Professor Beach
25 Horticulture Barn
26 Working Men's Cottage
27 Margaret Hall
28 Agricultural Engineering Hall
29 Horticulture Laboratory
30 Cattle Barn
31 Farm Stable
32 Upper Stock Judging Pavilion

33 Experiment Station Barn
34 Lower Stock Judging Pavilion
35 Central Heating Plant
36 Hall of Agriculture
37 Residence of Dean Curtiss
38 Dairy Building
39 Sheep Barn
40 Swine House
41 Residence of Mrs. Barrett
42 Residence of Professor Knapp
43 Residence of Professor Cessna
44 President's Residence, "The Knole"
45 Music Hall
46 Veterinary Hospital
53 Residence of Superintendent Sloss

1911 map of the college corresponding to features on the November 1867 survey map.
Bulletin, *Iowa State College of Agriculture and Mechanic Arts, Ames, Iowa, 10, No. 3 (December 1911)*

farms to cut timber, haul stone across the prairie from a local quarry, and make bricks for the house and barn. It was a true community effort at a time when most farmers had very little time or money to spare.

The trustees met on the farm in May 1860. Gaines took them on an inspection tour of the partially completed barn and house. He also presented them with a bill for his out-of-pocket expenses of $615 and another $146.12 in bills for the work on the house and barn. Gaines proudly reported that crops already were growing in some of the fields and would be ready for fall harvest. He expected the barn to be ready in the fall and the kitchen portion of the house to be completed soon after. The trustees left the college farm feeling confident that Gaines was doing a good job. They asked him to make regular progress reports and agreed to meet again on the farm in January 1861.

As winter closed in on the Iowa prairie, construction stopped on the buildings. The new barn stored the first harvest of the farm and provided shelter for the growing number of animals purchased by farm agent Gaines. The Farm House kitchen and washroom were essentially finished and ready for the trustees' visit and inspection in January.

The idea for a farmers' college was a new adventure for Iowans. These courageous people supported the notion that everyone should be given a chance at an education regardless of their financial situation. Lack of money, competition from the State University in Iowa City, and the start of the Civil War in 1861 challenged even the bravest of souls during the early years of the agricultural college.

3 · First Residents of the Farm House

*S*upporters of the agricultural college had every reason to be disillusioned during the early 1860s. Just months after the April 1861 start of the Civil War, old and young men alike left their Iowa farms behind and went off to fight. Few men remained on the farms and help was difficult to find. The state would not and could not provide any additional money for the agricultural college. It would take nine long years to get the first classroom building finished and the college open.

It was easy to travel past and miss the Farm House in early 1861. One traveler said that the prairie grasses grew so high that, even on horseback, he had difficulty locating the college farm and Farm House. The small redbrick story-and-a-half kitchen and attached wooden washroom stood alone on the rise of ground near the center of the farm. The only other building was a newly completed stone and wood barn northeast of the house on a sloping hillside. Debris left from work on the kitchen and barn littered the snow-covered ground. Work on the main portion of the house would begin again in the spring after the ground thawed.

All of the college trustees agreed to meet for a second time on the farm in early January 1861. Peter Melendy, a member of the trustees and a future superintendent of the farm, decided against traveling on horseback to the meeting and caught the stage in Cedar Falls. After an overnight stop in Nevada the stage continued west toward Boonesboro. Other trustees joined Melendy on the stage in Nevada and traveled with him across the frozen, bumpy roads to the college farm. To reach the Farm House, the stage made a sharp turn south from its regular route, practically forging its own road across the fields. This was not yet a regular stop on their route, but it was

Peter Melendy.
Courtesy of Iowa State University Library/University Archives

one that would soon become familiar to the stage drivers.

Richard Gaines, trustee and farm agent, met the new arrivals and showed them around the Farm House. He began with the cellar, which they planned to use for grain and vegetable storage. A doorway on the southeast end of the kitchen opened onto the cellar stairs, which were quite dark. The only light in the cellar came from the one window in the west wall and from a kerosene lamp provided by Gaines. The walls were thick stone, the floor was compacted black dirt. Above the stone walls workers laid rows of handmade red bricks, three deep, to form the upper walls of the kitchen. Thick handhewn beams supported the floors. The cellar was the same size as the kitchen, 16 feet wide and 24 feet long. It did not extend under the washroom. Satisfied with the condition of the foundation of the house, the trustees went back to the main floor and then up the narrow stairway to the second floor. A transom above the doorway to these stairs opened for ventilation in the summer.

The second-floor ceilings were only seven and one-half feet high and sloped to the east and west walls. There were three windows, one on the north wall and two on the west wall. Everything smelled new and the whitewash paint on the freshly plastered walls gave the rooms a stark, bright appearance. In the two rooms several crude, homemade beds were ready for the trustees, who would spend the night at the Farm House. Gaines also arranged for additional sleeping quarters at Washington Graham's home south of the college farm.

The tour of the house continued with a quick look at the main kitchen. Gaines pointed out the wood wainscoting installed around the room to prevent chipping of the plaster walls. The ceiling of this room was nine feet high. A large table with chairs took up the center of the room and the light from the two west windows was sufficient for reading or working. The trustees entered the washroom through a door in the north wall of the kitchen. This room also would be used to store wood and could be entered directly from the outside through a door on the south wall adjacent to the exterior kitchen door. The difference between the wooden washroom and the kitchen wing was obvious—the kitchen wing was built to withstand the cold Iowa winds, with 18-inch-thick exterior walls of red bricks. The one-story washroom would provide adequate storage but would be much harder to heat with its thin wooden walls.

It was bitterly cold outside so the farm tour continued with a fast walk to the barn located about 300 feet northeast of the Farm House. On their way to the barn, the trustees passed by the small orchard planted behind the house. Built on a sloping hillside, the barn, an impressive 42 feet wide and 60 feet long, was supported by beams and timber cut from white oak and black walnut trees that had grown on the farm. The shingles on the roofs of the barn and the Farm House also were from these trees. The upper level of the barn provided storage for the farm equipment and grains harvested the previous fall. Stone walls formed the foundation for the barn's lower level, which was eight feet high. This is where the stables and livestock pens were located. They opened to fields that were fenced in to keep the livestock from wandering away or entering the planted fields. Gaines expected that the 70 acres ready for spring planting would mean substantially more feed for the animals the next fall.

The official meeting began when everyone was back inside the Farm House kitchen. Mr. Gaines made his report on the status of the farm and then told the other trustees that he would not be able to continue as farm agent. This was no surprise to them as they were aware that Gaines had other obligations and his own farm had been neglected during the 18 months he had served as farm agent. Gaines told the trustees that someone needed to be living on the farm and he recommended renting the farm to one of the local farmers and tradesman, William Fitchpatrick of New Philadelphia. Fitchpatrick was familiar with the farm's operation and it was adjacent to his own 200-acre farm. With Gaines's recommendation, the trustees signed a two-year contract for the farm with Mr. Fitchpatrick for $200-a-year rent. The trustees also agreed to accept some of the crops Fitchpatrick harvested on the farm as partial payment of the rent. Fitchpatrick's contract began March 1, 1861, and continued through March 1, 1863. The contract allowed his family the use of the Farm House. Fitchpatrick was to look after all the farm animals and could bring to the farm his own team of oxen for breaking additional prairie he hoped to have ready for planting that spring.

William Fitchpatrick, Sr.
Farm House Museum Archives

Sarah Fitchpatrick (Mrs.
William).
Farm House Museum Archives

Joseph Fitchpatrick.
Farm House Museum Archives

It is not known for certain if the entire Fitchpatrick family moved to the Farm House in the spring of 1861. The family, with eight children, was living in New Philadelphia and probably had a cabin on their own farm just south of the college farm. The three eldest Fitchpatrick children were sons Joseph, age 21; William, 18; and John, 16. They helped their father in the store and on the farm. The five younger children were daughters Mary, age 13; Martha, 10; Sarah, 7; Nancy, 3; and baby Liza. The Fitchpatrick family was originally from Washington County, Virginia. They moved west to Indiana in 1842, then to Boone, Iowa, in 1854, and finally to New Philadelphia in western Story County in 1857. They liked Iowa and planned to stay.

News of the attack on the Union troops at Fort Sumter reached Story County within days of the April 1861 battle. The newspapers carried the story of the battle and a plea from President Lincoln for support to preserve the Union. Iowans were among the first to mobilize troops. Joseph Fitchpatrick began a diary in 1861; one of his first entries, dated May 1861 (no day listed), tells of his early involvement in the war. He wrote, "To Boone, enlisted in E. 3rd Iowa Infantry, then returned from Boone, planted corn."

The barn on the college farm became the scene of a hastily gathered group of young men who were leaving the area and enlisting in the army. A special stage stopped and picked them up on their way to Des Moines. Both William Fitchpatrick and his brother Joseph left the farm with the first groups of men to volunteer for army service. They spent the next four years in and out of battles and as prisoners of war in the notorious Southern Andersonville camp. Their younger brother, John, stayed on the farm to help their father but in August 1863, at the age of 18, he enlisted in the 8th Iowa Cavalry, Company I.

Without the help of his two older sons, William Fitchpatrick was unable to clear as many fields on the college farm as planned. John helped his father in the fields and the girls all worked with their mother keeping a garden and looking after the small animals on the farm. Mrs. Fitchpatrick also had her hands full keeping the children away from the workers who were now digging the cellar and erecting walls for the main portion of the Farm House. At this time, the Fitchpatricks lived in the finished part of the house, which consisted of the first-floor kitchen and the two small rooms upstairs.

Sarah Emery, ca. 1858. *Courtesy of Polly Gossard, from the Farwell Brown Photographic Collection, Ames Public Library*

During the day the children attended Hoggatt School and on warm days they could walk east across the fields and cross the Squaw Creek to get to school. The school stood near the present-day intersection of North Maple Street and Lincoln Way. The schoolteacher, Sarah Emery, received part of her salary in room and board supplied by the families of the children she taught. She boarded for part of the school year at the Farm House with the Fitchpatrick family. During 1862, the girls received several letters from their brother Joseph, who was now fighting in the South; he never failed to encourage the girls to keep up with their studies.

All three brothers survived their army experiences. Joseph returned to Story County after the war in 1866, married, and went into business for himself. William also returned to Story County but John moved to another state.

During the years the Fitchpatricks lived at the Farm House the mail stage from Nevada began to make a stop at the farm and William Fitchpatrick, Sr., took over the job as the first postmaster of the college farm. He or his son John would ride out to the north of the farm and meet the stage on its regular run to Boonesboro. The nearest neighbors could then collect their mail and newspapers at the farm. By 1864 a post office site was established in the small but growing community of Ames to the east.

The Fitchpatrick family moved from the college farm before the spring planting season of 1863 when their two-year contract expired.

They were not interested in renewing the contract since it had not been profitable for them and they returned to their own farm southeast of the college farm. The family prospered and later took in students as boarders after the college opened in 1869.

During the two years the Fitchpatricks lived on the college farm, the trustees were embroiled in a fierce battle for the very existence of the agricultural college. The one bright light in an otherwise gloomy financial future for the college was the federal legislation known as the Morrill Act, which provided land grants for the support of an agricultural college in each state of the Union. Naturally supporters of both the Iowa Agricultural College and the State University of Iowa fought over who should receive this major endowment. On September 11, 1862, the Iowa legislature accepted the provisions of the Morrill Act, which were very specific. To receive this land grant of 30,000 acres of federal land for each senator and representative in Congress in 1860, the state had to promise to maintain at least one college "where the leading object shall be, without excluding other scientific and classical studies, and including military tactics, to teach such branches of learning as are related to agriculture and the mechanic arts...to promote the liberal and practical education of the industrial classes in the several pursuits and professions in life."

The supporters of the State University of Iowa, hoping to secure the federal land grants for their own use, continued to lobby for the repeal of the legislation which established the Iowa Agricultural College. There was no need, they claimed, to duplicate what they believed could be handled at the State University. Besides, they pointed out rather smugly, the State University was now open to students and the Iowa Agricultural College was just a run-down farm with little to show for itself except a barn and a farmer's house. While the arguments raged on, Governor Kirkwood appointed Peter Melendy, a trustee of the Iowa Agricultural College, as the state's representative to select the federal lands in Iowa which would be used for an agricultural college. Melendy and his assistant spent three months traveling across the state examining the most desirable of the 6,000,000 acres of Iowa's federal lands before making their final selections.

In the fall of 1863, the trustees of the Iowa Agricultural College voted to create a new position on the board and appointed Peter Melendy the superintendent of the college farm. Melendy, they said, did an excellent job of selecting lands for the college and they created this position to show their appreciation for his good work. Although the decision as to whether they would actually receive the federal lands was still undecided, they were convinced they would prevail over the State University of Iowa.

Peter Melendy made his first visit to the college farm as superintendent in January 1864. The 90-mile trip from his home in Cedar Falls took him two days by stage and he was not in the best of humor when he arrived at the farm. What he saw greatly shocked him. No one had been living there since the Fitchpatricks moved from the farm months earlier. The Farm House, which was yet unfinished, was in disrepair. Tree limbs were damaged and were falling from the row of poplar trees planted by Fitchpatrick as windbreaks. Weeds and remnants of old crops covered the farm fields. A brief inventory showed numerous pieces of farm equipment missing. Intruders had apparently pilfered grain from the barn and had left tell-tale trails through the adjacent fields. Melendy suspected itinerant railroad workers had taken the grain and tools. Since the railroad had begun laying tracks through the east portion of the college farm in 1863, reports of vandalism in the county were on the rise.

Melendy had no intention of living on the farm even though the trustees wanted the superintendent to do so. He made it clear when he accepted the position that he would be hiring a manager to look after the daily activities of the farm. Melendy planned to spend time at the farm directing its actual development but would continue to live at his home in Cedar Falls.

Before Melendy returned to Cedar Falls, he convinced Washington T. Graham to look after the farm until Melendy could hire a permanent farm manager. Melendy hoped to have a manager on the farm before the spring planting season. He already knew he would offer the farm manager's job to his business partner, Andrew J. Graves. Melendy wasn't certain Graves would take the job because it meant moving his wife, who was expecting a child, from their comfortable home in Cedar Falls to a house in dreadful condition in the middle of the prairie. Graves, who preferred to be called "A. J." by his business associates, formed a partnership with Melendy in the early 1860s to supply plows, corn planters, and reapers to farmers around Cedar Falls. Graves was also an agent for the Dubuque nurseries and solicited subscriptions for a farm magazine. Before settling in Iowa in 1858, Graves had moved from his native Vermont to California, where he had enjoyed success as a businessman and schoolmaster. Shortly after his arrival in Iowa, he married Mary M. Meredith and after six years of marriage they were now expecting their first child in the summer of 1864.

Melendy notified the trustees of his choice for farm manager and received their approval. They offered Graves a four-year contract for his services and gave him the use of the Farm House as partial payment. His contract began on April 19, 1864, and continued through April 19, 1868.

Before Graves even arrived at the college farm, the Iowa legislature decided the fate of the federal endowment of lands for an agricultural college. On March 29, 1864, the state of Iowa awarded the lands acquired under the Morrill Act to the Iowa Agricultural College and Model Farm in Story County. This was not without a fight. The State University of Iowa, realizing that they were losing the battle, asked the legislature to divide the lands equally between their university and the college in Story County. Fortunately for the fledgling Iowa State Agricultural College, this did not happen. Once the final decision was made, Benjamin Gue, Governor Kirkwood, and Senator C. F. Clarkson proposed that the lands not be put up for immediate sale because they knew these lands would be in competition with other available land and would, therefore, bring a lower selling price. Instead, they recommended that the individual parcels of land be rented for periods of 10 years at 8 percent of their appraised value. At the end of the 10 years, the renter could either renew the lease or purchase the lands. In this way, the Iowa Agricultural College and Model Farm received a permanent source of revenue that paid most of the college bills through the 1890s.

Graves packed his family belongings in a wagon and headed for the college farm about April 10, 1864. It took him eight days to travel the rough, muddy 90 miles from Cedar Falls to Story County. Mary Graves followed her husband several days later and made the trip in two days on the stage. Graves arrived at the college farm on April 19, 1864. His first impression of the Farm House was one of dismay. Melendy had warned him that the house needed work, but Graves did not expect he would be doing most of it himself. He found few finished walls in the main front part of the house and those that were finished needed painting. Mere bare wood studs gave shape to many of the rooms. He was also shocked that the Farm House, with its four chimneys, did not have a single fireplace. The only sources of heat were two potbellied stoves on the main floor.

Graves soon spoke with Washington T. Graham about the condition of the farm. Graham told him that help was nearly impossible to find because of the war but that he would try to help Graves hire a farm crew. Graves also discovered that the tools he ordered had not

arrived. Graham did manage to find several field workers for Graves who offered them room and board at the
Farm House as partial payment for their work. With the
help of these men, Graves cleared the fields and planted
22 acres of wheat and 22 acres of oats. Graves was
pleased when the shipment of 10,000 evergreen trees he
had ordered before leaving Cedar Falls finally arrived.
The trees were planted to provide a windbreak for the
house and barns.

When Graves wasn't in the fields, he was working
on the Farm House. He made weekly trips to the local
sawmill to buy wood lath (which he put up himself) for
the interior walls of the house. He also plastered and
painted the walls. It took him a year to finish the inside
of the house.

Andrew J. Graves.
Farm House Museum Archives

It's difficult to imagine how Mary Graves kept
house under such formidable conditions. Plaster dust
floated through the air, the smell of fresh paint could
make one sick, and there certainly was little privacy.
Mary also cooked meals for everyone working at the
farm. The one small convenience was fresh water supplied by the well just outside the back door of the
house. Exactly when the doorway to the kitchen wing
was opened to the main section of the house is not
clear. It is possible that the Graves family used the
kitchen wing and bedrooms above for their personal
use and boarded the farmhands in the unfinished front
part of the house during the first summer they lived
there. On July 27, 1864, Mary Graves gave birth to her
first child, Edward. The Farm House would be home to
Edward until he was four years old.

Mary Graves (Mrs. Andrew J.).
Farm House Museum Archives

With the college farm now in good hands, the
trustees developed the plans for the main college building, which they hoped to complete by 1866. They
awarded the first contract for the building in the summer of 1864. The building was to be located across a
wide expanse of prairie west of the Farm House and the
fields under cultivation. The construction crews moved
into the one-story wooden temporary housing units

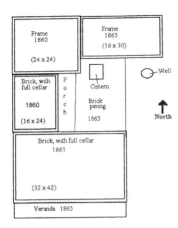

Computer-generated image
of the Farm House in 1868.
*Adapted from drawing by H.
Summerfield Day, 1980, in* The
Iowa State University Campus
and Its Buildings, 1859-1879

built near the building site. Problems with the bricks
for the building developed almost immediately. They
were made right on the farm, as were the bricks for the
Farm House, but since they had not been properly
fired they were soft and crumbled easily. The trustees
discharged the original contractor and secured another
firm to finish the building. Money for the building
came from an appropriation from the Iowa legislature,
whose members were not pleased to hear of the delays
caused by faulty workmanship.

Peter Melendy and A. J. Graves worked well together to develop the college farm. In 1865, Melendy
made 10 trips to the farm and spent over 135 days on
college farm business. Graves's duties as farm manager
encompassed a wide variety of responsibilities. By his
own account, he hauled sand and more than 100,000
bricks from the brickyard to the college building site.

With the end of the Civil War in April 1865,
Iowans began returning to their farms. Slowly the
number of people looking for work increased and
Graves was able to hire more help for the farm. Graves

The front of the Farm House, ca. 1870s. The porch had been added in
1865.
Courtesy of Iowa State University Library/University Archives

directed the digging of ditches around the farm fields to control
drainage and prevent flood damage to the crops that now provided
food for the livestock and for those living at the Farm House. Mary
kept a garden close by the house and planted potatoes, turnips, car-
rots, and cabbage for the table. She tried to store vegetables in the
cellar under the kitchen but it was too damp during most of the year.
Graves laid tile in the basement to drain off the water hoping to make
it usable for storage of vegetables and grain. He also whitewashed
the walls and ceilings in the cellar to help seal them against moisture.

Graves continued to make improvements to the Farm House. In
1865, he worked on a porch for the front of the house. It extended
the full width of the house and provided a pleasant place to sit and
talk in the warm spring sunshine. It also softened the rather stark appearance of the house. The shape and size of the Farm House
changed with the addition of another single-story wooden workshop
attached to the east side of the washroom. The shape of the house
now resembled a squared "C." The workshop, 18 feet wide and 30
feet long, had shuttered windows and whitewashed walls. It was di-
vided in the center; one side provided storage for wood and the other
was a workshop and room for the farmhands to spend their leisure
hours in, if they had any. Behind the workshop they built a 12-foot

FARM HOUSE & BARNS

View of the west side of the farm buildings and the Farm House
(*right*). The privy and smokehouse are to the left of the house.
A. T. Andreas, Illustrated Atlas of the State of Iowa, *1875*

View of the east side of the farm buildings, ca. 1875.
Etching in Iowa Agricultural College Catalogue. *Courtesy of Iowa State University Library/University Archives*

brick smoke and ash house and a 10-foot square brick privy with plastered walls.

Melendy served as farm superintendent during 1864 and 1865 but declined to serve another year. His final report to the trustees included an accounting of the number of cattle, ewes, pigs, turkeys, and chickens now at the college farm. Melendy also complimented A. J. Graves for the work he was doing and reported on some of the experiments he did relating to crop rotation, fertilizers, and new varieties of seeds. Melendy also mentioned a growing problem with the railroads, whose tracks extended from the eastern border of the farm, through the center and up through the northwest corner. He found it necessary to hire someone full time just to keep the cattle from the tracks and to put out fires started by sparks from the trains.

Melendy's replacement as superintendent was a fellow trustee, Moses W. Robinson. Robinson operated a farm near Des Moines and was one of the early supporters of the agricultural college. He was also involved early on with plans for the college building. Robinson accepted a one-year contract as superintendent of the farm for a yearly salary of $1,000 plus the use of the Farm House for his family. He also could keep a team of his own horses or oxen on the farm and feed his family from any crops or meat butchered there. The trustees requested that Robinson begin his duties and be on the farm by March 1, 1866.

Robinson arrived at the Farm House without his family. He decided against bringing them because they were needed on their own farm about 35 miles south of the college farm. Apparently, Moses Robinson and the Graves family got along reasonably well living together at the Farm House. Mrs. Graves was now accustomed to a very busy household which included her own family, the farmhands, and frequent visitors to the farm. The trustees often held their marathon meetings at the Farm House and required sleeping accommodations for several nights. Everyone knew when the trustees were in session because of all the cigar smoke.

Mrs. Graves found it necessary to hire help from local farm families to keep up with the demand for hot meals and clean beds. Originally, there were seven bedrooms on the second floor including the kitchen wing. (Two small adjoining bedrooms were merged in 1867.) The third floor was finished and may have been one large dormitory-style room, later converted to two bedrooms. Rarely was a bedroom empty because this was the only housing at the college (other than the temporary housing for the construction crews). The rooms were furnished with the barest essentials purchased from college funds. Mrs. Graves was permitted to charge room and board to visitors to help defray expenses. Meals were $.50 and a week's room and board was $3.50. Visitors to the college could buy a hot meal, sit and read the newspaper in the farm office, and discuss local politics with the farm staff. In this way, the Farm House took on the character of an English tavern, which may be where the stories about the house actually having been a tavern originated.

On July 11, 1866, Superintendent Robinson began a daily journal which he called the *College Farm Journal*. He wrote about daily life on the farm, what the farmhands were doing, and what crops were planted and harvested. A three-acre garden continued to provide potatoes, sorghum, buckwheat, and other vegetables for the Farm House kitchen. Marigolds, planted to keep the bugs away from the vegetables, added color to the dinner table. During the hot August days of 1866, the farmhands hauled manure to the fields from the barn and fought off bugs that were attacking the crops. Workers also hauled sand and bricks from the brickyard and installed a brick floor in the Farm House cellar. In September, fall plowing and butchering began.

The trustees met at the Farm House at least three times during 1866, principally to discuss the plan and construction schedule for the main college building. They were being pressured by the Iowa legislature to get the college open. Graves was told to release the farmhands for half of their day so they could help with the college building. Graves found himself working on the Main Building as well. To complicate matters, Superintendent Robinson resigned from his position that fall. He assured the trustees that he would remain until December to complete the year's service. He did say, however, that this arrangement did not work for him or his family and that he was needed at home.

The arrival of Robinson's replacement, Hugh Thomson, was the beginning of trouble for the Graves family at the Farm House. Thomson served in the Iowa legislature and was a vocal supporter of the Iowa Agricultural College. He had a reputation as a "gruff, big-hearted Scotsman." He was also an excellent farmer.

Thomson arrived at the farm on January 24, 1867, in time to attend the trustees' first meeting of the year. At this meeting, Peter Melendy, Governor William Stone, and Benjamin Gue, who was now lieutenant governor, formed a committee to select the faculty for the college. The trustees asked the committee to visit other agricultural colleges in the country and devise a course of study which would work in Iowa. They also hoped to attract a highly capable faculty. Stone was unable to leave his legislative duties so Melendy and Gue prepared to visit the schools and talk with prospective faculty.

Thomson began his work on the farm during a bitterly cold winter. He continued the daily record of the *College Farm Journal* started by the former superintendent. Thomson frequently mentioned the terrible weather, which prevented any work from being done outside except, as he noted, "getting stock to water." It was during this early period of close confinement that Thomson and the Graves family developed a distinct dislike for each other. Mrs. Graves was offended by Thomson's brusque manner and A. J. Graves resented Thomson's way of ordering him about. Graves had a different relationship with the former superintendents and much more freedom to do his own work. Thomson, like Robinson, did not bring his family to the Farm House and made frequent trips home because his family seemed constantly to be in a state of ill health. Graves felt Thomson spent too much time away from the farm and thought his service to the college "questionable."

Spring weather wasn't much better. Cold and rainy days delayed planting until early June. When Thomson ordered Graves to work in the fields with the other farmhands to get the crops planted, Graves refused, saying that he was hired to look after the farm not work as a field hand. Graves's last year on the farm would not be an easy one.

During his last year, Graves installed skylights for ventilation in the east roof of the kitchen ell of the Farm House. He built one skylight directly over the stairway and the other in the north bedroom. These skylights remained in use until the early 1970s when workers removed them while making roof repairs. He also tore down the false ceiling in a small bedroom on the second floor and removed the wall between that room and the adjacent room to create one L-shaped room. It is the only bedroom in the house with two doors onto the hallway and a transom above one of the doors.

One of Graves's last official duties before he left the college farm took place at the State Fair in Des Moines. He and Mr. Miller, one of the farmhands, selected the best sheep and swine from the livestock and proudly exhibited them at the fair. Whether Graves took back to the college any blue ribbons is not certain.

While Graves completed his final year on the farm, Peter Melendy and Benjamin Gue pursued candidates for the faculty. In 1867, they made their recommendation to the trustees for their choice of a curriculum for the college and a president who they believed had the right credentials, experience, and energy to head the new agricultural college. More importantly, they wanted someone who was not afraid to take the risk of heading a small, developing college out on the prairie.

After visiting over 16 agricultural schools and colleges and the Smithsonian Institution in Washington, D.C., and talking with members of the federal Departments of Agriculture and Education, they settled on a course of study and school program similar to the one at Michigan Agricultural College, which they considered to be the top agricultural program in the nation. They received an abundance of recommendations for the president's position and for faculty for the college. Their choice for president was Adonijah Welch, a graduate of the University of Michigan, who in the 1850s served as principal of the State Normal School where the emphasis was on industrial education. President Abbot of Michigan Agricultural College gave Welch a glowing endorsement. At the time, however, Welch was living in

Adonijah S. Welch.
Courtesy of Iowa State University Library/University Archives

Hugh Muir Thomson, ca. 1886.
Courtesy of Guy D. McCubbin

Florida and serving in the U.S. Senate. It took some doing to convince Welch to accept the presidency of the Iowa Agricultural College.

It was May 1868 before Welch finally agreed to come to Iowa with the understanding that he could complete his term in the U.S. Senate, which ended in March 1869. The trustees agreed to pay Welch $3,000 a year and to provide him with a home on the college grounds. The trustees completed the faculty by hiring Albert E. Foote, professor of chemistry, Norton S. Townshend (Townsend), professor of practical agriculture, and George W. Jones, professor of mathematics.

Now that a faculty was in place for the college, the trustees were doubly anxious to get the Main Building finished. They weren't certain what they would do if it wasn't ready in September when the first group of students were expected for the preliminary session. At least the college farm was prospering and developing into the model farm they all had envisioned.

To the surprise of the college trustees, Superintendent Thomson offered his resignation in February 1868. He told them he felt it was necessary due "in consequence of some representation of dissatisfaction with my conduct." The trustees refused to accept his resignation in the hope that things would settle down for Thomson after Graves left the farm.

In April 1868, after four years as farm manager, A. J. Graves packed his family's furniture and personal possessions and prepared to move from the Farm House. He and his wife, Mary, liked living in Story County. In 1865 they had purchased from the college land agent a large tract of land southeast of the college and they planned to work their own farm. Graves later became a successful businessman in Ames and served from 1903 until 1911 as the first president of the Ames Savings Bank.

Thomson's terse entry in the *College Farm Journal* gives us an exact date of Graves's departure: "April 10, 1868....Graves time being at a close as provided by his contract he is attending to his own business." The very next day, Graves's replacement arrived at the farm. Thomson had given careful consideration to his selection of a new farm manager. He did not want a repeat of the unpleasant scenes that took place between himself and Graves.

The new farm manager was a young farmer, James Gilmore. He and his wife, Eliza, had four sons—John, George, Jamie, and Robert—aged ten, eight, six, and four. It was agreed that Mrs. Gilmore would look after the house and boarders. Payment for her services was included in her husband's salary. Officially she was the Farm House matron in charge of cooking and housekeeping. Unofficially she did just about everything that needed doing around the house while trying to maintain a home for her young children. She cared for the kitchen garden, canned vegetables for use later in the season, collected firewood for the stoves, and ran a kitchen which often served 15 to 30 people for meals, depending on the number of farmhands, visitors, or trustees who were staying at the house.

Under orders from the trustees, Thomson continued to send the farmhands to work on the college building for half of each day. The farmhands also helped build bridges over the small streams running through the farm and dug ditches to drain the water away from the road. Much of the area south of the construction site of the main college building and Farm House was marshland. Consequently the roads leading into the college grounds were constantly flooding and washing out. It was a common occurrence to see wagons loaded with brick, lumber, and other building supplies stuck deep in the black mud.

The new farm manager joined the construction crews when he could manage time away from his duties. He first spent time just getting used to the daily farm routine, which on a single day could take him to the fields to repair fencing, fight off grasshoppers, and help spread the manure carried from the barns for fertilizer while trying to get the spring planting completed. His oldest son, John, often accompanied him around the farm and did his own share of work. The younger boys helped their mother with the garden and did their share of farm chores.

By September 1868, the Main Building was nearing completion. It would, however, take several years to make it habitable. It was an impressive structure with its Mansard roofs. It housed the dining hall, all of the classrooms, and dormitory rooms for the students. It did not, however, have plumbing or provisions for gas lighting, and the Rutan furnace, which was heralded as one of the modern marvels of the world, was a miserable failure. The students who arrived early for

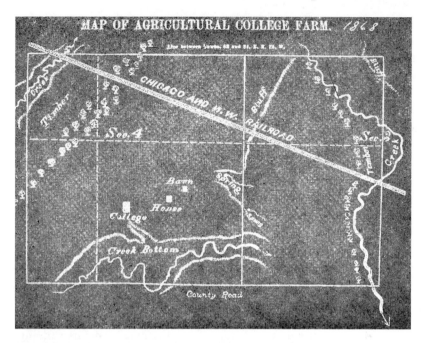

Map of Agricultural College and Model Farm, 1868.
Courtesy of Iowa State University Library/University Archives

the October session soon found themselves driving wagons hauling
wood and coal to the college building or meeting the train in Ames
to pick up furniture intended for the classrooms and dining hall.

President-elect Welch's first wife died in 1866, leaving him to
care for three young children. Before leaving Florida, Welch married
Mary Dudley, the widow of a former friend, who had one young
daughter, Winifred. This was the family that arrived at the college on
a cold, wet day in late September 1868. One of the local farmers who
was in town offered the Welch family a ride to the campus from the
Ames train station since there was no one there to meet them from
the college. The Welch family and their suitcases were piled into the
wagon for the trip to the college. Mrs. Welch was extremely tired from
the trip and the four children were anxious about their new home. As
the wagon entered the college grounds, Welch saw to his dismay that
his house was still under construction. When the wagon pulled up to
the Farm House, the only one there to greet the new president was
Superintendent Thomson.

The memory of their arrival at the Farm House was still fresh in
Winifred Dudley's mind 30 years later when she recounted her first
impressions of the Farm House as a ten-year-old. She wrote:

I think I can recall every article of furniture in that room [the office on the northwest corner of the house]....A long office table with heavy wooden chairs around it, a dirty inkstand and some disreputable looking pens, a newspaper or two, and some state reports, and a big thermometer. The floor was bare save for the muddy tracks of workmen's boots, and the air was heavy with stale tobacco smoke. The rest of the Farm House was as unfurnished and dreary, but in one of its upper rooms, uncarpeted and half-heated, with two beds, and the barest necessaries of chairs and washstand, Dr. Welch wrote his inaugural address.

Mary Beaumont Dudley Welch (Mrs. Adonijah S.). *Courtesy of Iowa State University Library/University Archives*

Dr. Welch stayed at the college just long enough to see that his family was settled in the Farm House before leaving for Washington, D.C., to complete his term in Congress. The three other faculty members arrived at the college before Welch headed east. Welch's wife, Mary, an experienced teacher, took over his classes during the preliminary session which began immediately in October. The preliminary session was designed specially for students who were not yet ready for college courses and who needed some quick way of helping them make the transition. Seventy-five students signed up for this session, nine of them women.

Mary Welch and the children boarded at the Farm House through November, then they moved into rooms in the Main Building. With eight children in the house, there had been no end of noise and confusion. Both Mrs. Welch and Mrs. Gilmore had been under a great deal of strain. In addition to Mary Welch and the four Welch children, the Gilmore family of six, and Superintendent Thomson, the Farm House was temporary home to three professors—Albert Foote, Norton Townshend, and George Jones. How many farmhands or kitchen help lived at the house during this time isn't known. The Farm House was still the only housing available except for the Main Building, so it is reasonable to assume they continued to board at the Farm House.

Practically everyone disliked the new building for one reason or another. When the Welch children moved over there, they expected conditions to be better than

Winifred Dudley Shaw. Reminiscenses of Iowa Agricultural College, 1897

they had been at the Farm House. But small tallow candles provided the only lighting and the privy was a long walk behind the building. Just keeping warm was a challenge. It was so cold inside the new building that the children were forced to wear coats and mittens during the day to keep warm. Superintendent Thomson wrote only one sentence in the *College Farm Journal* on Christmas Day, 1868: "4 students Brown, Cadwell, Anderson and Cessna hauled coal to the College all day both teams."

The preliminary session concluded the first week of January 1869. Some of the students stayed at the college to help with the work but most returned home until the official opening of the college, planned for March 17, 1869. Work on the building and farm came to a stop because of the continual snowstorms and blowing, drifting snow. The farmhands found themselves working indoors and spent most of their time fixing and oiling harnesses, hoping spring would soon arrive. At least the workshop attached to the Farm House washroom provided space where the farmhands could work during the day away from the main house.

Not much could be done on the farm during January and February except watering and feeding the livestock. Gilmore did manage to get some wheat and bran to the mill to replenish the dwindling supply of flour in the college kitchen.

The trustees held their first meeting of 1869 in Des Moines on January 11. Hugh Thomson accepted another one-year contract as farm superintendent. The trustees encouraged Thomson to continue experimenting with new planting schedules and the use of different crops on the farm. Thomson kept detailed records in the *College Farm Journal* of all the crops planted on the farm. Soon he would have a fresh supply of eager young students looking to him for guidance in their work on the farm.

The official opening of the college took place on March 17, 1869. The trustees arrived the day before, some spending the night at the Farm House and some at the Main Building. Crowds of visitors and dignitaries began arriving on the college grounds early in the morning and waited for the ceremony to begin. The railroads issued passes and special trains stopped at the college to deliver most of the estimated 1,200 visitors for the event. Not everyone arrived by train, most of the local people came by wagon or horseback to attend the afternoon ceremony, which took place in front of the Main Building.

Lieutenant Governor Scott addressed the crowd and welcomed

them to the college. Benjamin Gue, now president of the Board of Trustees, reminisced about the beginning of the college in which he was intimately involved. Governor Merrill presented the charter and seal to President-elect Welch and the Honorable John Russell presented Welch with the keys to the Main Building. Welch's inaugural speech was as timely then as it would be today. He was eloquent and spoke of the need for a practical industrial education for both men and women, which he intended to see that the college provided. He congratulated everyone who helped make the college a reality and praised their efforts in "extending to a large class of students opportunities of which they have been hitherto, in great measure unjustly deprived." Professor Norton Townshend replied to the president's remarks by saying: "We are also in fullest sympathy with the provision made here for the education of woman....It is hard to see why she does not need and deserve an equal education."

At the conclusion of the ceremony the college officially opened its doors. Iowa Agricultural College and Model Farm became the first coeducational land-grant school in the country. Ten years elapsed between the Fourth of July picnic celebrating the location of the new college and the formal opening of the college in 1869. During these 10 years, the nation survived a Civil War and the Iowa Agricultural College survived numerous assaults on its very existence. The site for the college was a most improbable one—in the middle of a wild prairie surrounded by dense, wet marshes. Now, with a sound financial endowment provided by the federal Morrill Act, many had high hopes for the future of the college under the leadership of its first president, Adonijah Welch.

4 · First Years of the College: 1869–1879

*T*he State Agricultural College and Model Farm opened its doors for business on March 17, 1869, with 173 bewildered students, half of whom required remedial classes; four eager faculty who made up the textbooks from their notes; and one partially finished college building that served as dormitory, dining room, chapel, and classroom. The Farm House was well established on the east side of the campus and provided a temporary haven from the turmoil in the Main Building. Every afternoon students descended on the farm anxious to find work that would satisfy the college's manual labor requirement and at the same time give them pocket money to help pay their expenses at the college. Tuition was free but every student was required to work two to three hours a day, five days a week, for which they received up to 10 cents an hour. The superintendent of the farm was responsible for planning the students' farm work schedules and for seeing that they were all employed. He grew increasingly resentful of the added responsibilities imposed upon him when the college opened and within six months of that date, he resigned. It was the beginning of a series of problems that Dr. Welch and the trustees faced during those first critical years of the college.

Shortly after the college opened in March 1869, the Welch family moved back to the Farm House, relinquishing their rooms in Main Building for the students. Ten-year-old Winifred, Welch's daughter, later wrote that the Farm House seemed much more pleasant to her in the spring and any unhappy memory of the half-heated, barren bedrooms in the Farm House the previous fall was soon forgotten. The fact that the president of the college lived at the Farm House did not seem to make much difference in the daily routine of the house,

65

and there was little time to worry about formalities. The Farm House was still the farm office and a boarding house and the president's family was treated just like everyone else.

The original plan of the trustees was to provide all the faculty with on-campus housing and three homes were begun in 1868 near the Main Building. Winifred recalled the family was having breakfast at the Farm House when a worker came running in to tell them that the brick walls on their house and the other professors' houses had collapsed. The bricks from this disaster found their way into pavement and the house construction began again. That was the reason the faculty found themselves sharing the Farm House in the spring of 1869. Dr. Foote was a bachelor and needed only one room, but Dr. Townshend brought his wife with him and Dr. Jones, who was acting president during the fall when Welch was away, also brought his wife and two daughters to the college. Two of the houses were promised to Dr. Welch and Dr. Jones. The third house might have been intended for Dr. Townshend but he left the college before it was finished. Dr. Foote found the accommodations at the Farm House satisfactory and planned to stay there indefinitely.

When dinnertime rolled around there were often 30 people to feed, including Superintendent Thomson and Mr. and Mrs. Gilmore and their four children. More than one room must have been set with tables and the children might have been served first to make room for the adults. Mary Welch was a marvelous cook and she probably offered culinary advice to Mrs. Gilmore. Mary's recipes became the basis for a cookbook she later used while teaching domestic economy at the college.

During the preliminary session the previous fall, Superintendent Thomson made all the work assignments, but with the opening of the college, Dr. Welch preferred to do this himself. Thomson would relay the daily farm schedule to Dr. Welch, who would meet with student leaders each day after lunch to hand out the day's work assignments. Not everyone worked on the farm; some worked on the college grounds or in the Main Building in housekeeping or for one of the faculty. Those students who worked on the farm organized into squads of 6 to 20 people. Each squad leader would get their crew together after Dr. Welch handed out the jobs for the day, then they would report to the farm and Superintendent Thomson. It was Thomson's job to see that the students were kept busy. This was not always possible because of uncooperative weather.

While the students needed to work, not all of them were excited about the manual labor they were doing because it really did not offer them practical experience that would help them find a good job after college. To the disappointment of their parents, most of the students didn't plan to return to farm work, which was hard and dirty. During that first school year, some of the students left before completing even one session and others arrived to take their places. By the end of the first year, there were 192 students enrolled in the remedial sessions and regular college classes, and dormitory rooms in the Main Building were full.

In September 1869, just six months after the opening of the college, Superintendent Thomson complained to the trustees that he was spending so much time working on the college building and the campus roads that he couldn't look after the farm properly. Earlier in the month, Thomson discovered that students had removed wood from the fencing around the fields to use as fuel in the Main Building. President Welch had little sympathy for the freezing students and called it a willful waste and extravagance. Thomson blamed himself for not being there to prevent the fences from disappearing and was concerned that the livestock would wander away or get onto the railroad tracks.

That was just one in a series of incidents that finally prompted Thomson to resign. His reason, he wrote to the trustees, was the continued escalation of his nonfarm duties. After two and one-half years at the college Thomson made his last entry in the *College Farm Journal* on September 30, 1869; it consisted of a statement of his dissatisfaction with his job and ended with, "thus ends my official connection with the Iowa Agricultural College." The following day, Thomson packed up his personal possessions and left the Farm House.

The trustees believed that Thomson just needed a short leave from the college and they waited until December to offer him the superintendent's position for the coming year, 1870. In the meantime, the farm manager, James Gilmore, took over the student scheduling with Dr. Welch's help. At first Thomson completely rejected the idea of returning to the college but he finally relented when the trustees agreed to his demands that he not be asked to purchase any supplies for the Main Building nor work on anything unrelated to the farm. However, before Thomson could return to the college he and the trustees got into more arguments over his duties and he resigned again. This time the exasperated trustees gladly released Thomson from any further commitment to the college. Finding a replacement for Thomson, however, would not be easy.

In the fall of 1869, Dr. Welch moved his family from the Farm House into their new two-story campus home located a short walk south of the Main Building and east of where Union and Morrill roads now intersect. Dr. Jones's house, which was across the road and west of Dr. Welch's home, was ready by April 1870. The third faculty house was also finished by the 1870 spring session and was assigned to a new faculty member, Professor Anthony. The house originally may have been intended for Dr. Townshend but he returned to Ohio, where he took a similar position in the Ohio agricultural college which he had helped to establish. The only one of the four original faculty members to remain at the Farm House was Dr. Foote, who continued living there for several years.

After the various faculty members moved from the Farm House, the company of boarders was quite diverse. In 1870, Nicholas Stark, head carpenter for the president's house, his wife, and ten-year-old son boarded at the Farm House, along with John Radford and Robert McCarey, carpenters; Christian Petersen, farmhand; and Augusta Mathews, music teacher. Mrs. Gilmore did her best to cope. She employed two young women, Lizzie Williams and Mary Lewis, to help in the kitchen. They also boarded at the Farm House. After school, Mrs. Gilmore's four sons ran errands, kept the wood pile stacked, and helped clean the kerosene lamps. The older boys helped their dad in the garden and often tracked in thick black mud, as did the students and fieldhands. Mud seemed to be everywhere, and the floors of the Farm House were seldom clean for very long.

In May 1870, the trustees placed Dr. Welch in charge of the farm until a suitable candidate could be found for the superintendent's job. In the spring of 1870, Mr. O. H. P. Buchanan, an enterprising member of the college trustees, began his own search for a farm superinten-dent. He had his eye on a Mount Pleasant farmer, Isaac Phillips Roberts. Buchanan made a special trip to talk with Roberts about the position. Buchanan's arrival was totally unexpected and he found Roberts working on the roof of his barn. Roberts remembered later how Buchanan shouted up to him to get down from the ladder be-cause he had more important business to discuss with him than building a barn. When Buchanan first asked him to consider the su-perintendent's job, Roberts rejected it. But Buchanan was so persua-sive and made the college sound so attractive that Roberts finally agreed to be considered for the position. It was Buchanan's recom-mendation that convinced the trustees to hire Roberts.

Roberts was surprised when the trustees formally offered him the position. When he accepted their offer, he was even more surprised that they wanted him to begin work immediately. He hastily arranged for someone to stay at his farm and help his wife while he was gone. His biggest regret, he later wrote, was not doing one day of work in the new barn he had just completed. Roberts was at the college farm just long enough to get the harvest in before returning home to do the same at his own farm. He really believed that he and his family would be away from their farm for just a year or so. Accordingly he made arrangements to rent the farm and house while they were gone. Mr. and Mrs. Roberts stored most of their furniture in the upstairs rooms of their house and brought only those items needed for a short stay at the college farm.

Isaac P. Roberts.
Courtesy of Iowa State University Library/University Archives

Earlier in the year, the trustees had purchased a farm which bordered on the north edge of the college grounds. They offered Mr. Gilmore the manager's position after Mr. Roberts accepted the superintendent's job at the college. A small house on the north farm was quite suitable for the Gilmores and they moved into it to make room at the Farm House for the Roberts family. The use of the house was included in Mr. Gilmore's pay. After two and one-half years at the Farm House, with a constant procession of boarders coming and going, this was a pleasant change for the family. That fall Mr. Gilmore received an extra bonus plus his regular wages to help with the expenses of moving his family. He continued to work for the college for a number of years and was still on the north farm in May 1877 when his salary was raised from $25 a month to $33.33 a month plus housing.

Roberts began his duties as superintendent of the college farm and secretary of the Board of Trustees in August 1870. Although Roberts states in his book, *Autobiography of a Farm Boy,* that he arrived on the farm in August 1869, the date he signed his contract and began writing in the Board of Trustees' minutes was actually August 1870. His salary of $1,750 a year included payment to his wife, Margaret, for her services as housekeeper at the Farm House. They also received free room and board, heat, light, and washing privileges. Roberts wrote in his autobiography that he "superintended" the farm and his wife "superintended" the Farm House.

It was a difficult adjustment for Mrs. Roberts, who gave up a happy, contended life to suddenly be thrown into the middle of a noisy, bustling household. She agreed to be responsible for the housekeeping duties at the Farm House to help her husband but she never really enjoyed it. She was the daughter of a wealthy farmer in Kingsbury, Indiana, when she married Isaac Roberts in 1857. They moved to Mount Pleasant, Iowa, in 1862, after their daughter was born. There they bought a large acreage and built the home where their son was born. They were very comfortably situated on the farm when Mr. Roberts accepted the position at the college.

Mrs. Roberts soon found that, for all its size, the Farm House lacked privacy. There was really nowhere to be alone since the boarders shared the parlor and dining areas and the bedrooms were often shared by family members. The front porch was a pleasant place to sit and converse but it was open to the road and the dust, which blew across the fields. The one cool spot in the hot summertime where Mrs. Roberts could sit with the children was the brick courtyard outside the kitchen door. Fortunately, the farmhands avoided the main house as much as possible and used the workhouse as a place to work or play cards.

Mr. Roberts's autobiography offers us an interesting picture of the Farm House as he saw it when he first arrived. He wrote:

> I remember that the kitchen door, which faced on what was then the main drive, opened on the very line of the road. The wood for the stoves had been deposited in saw-log lengths at the kitchen door to be chopped up into stove lengths.

When Dr. Welch took over the farm, he began to see the potential for a separate Department of Agriculture Studies. He convinced the trustees to make the farm a department of the college. Dr. Welch was very impressed with Roberts's handling of the farm and asked him to take over the lectures in agriculture. Even though Roberts lacked a college education, Welch had great faith in his ability to teach at the college. Roberts was a graduate of the Seneca Falls Academy in New York and read prodigiously. During the winters when he wasn't working on his farm he had even taught at the local school in Mt. Pleasant. Dr. Welch told Roberts he should "just tell the boys how you have been doing things." When Roberts couldn't find any suitable books on practical agriculture he began taking the students into the fields for what he called "walks and talks." Later he took the students on road trips on open freight cars so they could see examples of good and bad farms as they traveled throughout the county. He and Dr. Welch used a similar idea to begin a series of farmers' institutes in 1870 that later developed into the county extension system.

The trustees promoted Roberts to professor of agriculture before he completed his first year at the college. Roberts later attributed his success to his campaign to clean up the college grounds. In his autobiography he wrote a vivid account of the scene on the campus:

> From forty to fifty [students] were detailed...to the farm...I decided to clear up the campus. Heterogeneous rubbish due to many changes and much building was gathered in wagon loads, sorted and piled up. The knotty logs at the kitchen door were moved...and the vast accumulation of chip manure was hauled away which widened the drive-way from about twelve to its original forty feet.

He also put the students to work mowing the east pasture, which was the main entrance to the college from Ames. He wrote that the weeds were so high he couldn't see the grazing cattle. He also thought the unsightly fields left a bad impression on visitors.

In 1871, Roberts converted the two east rooms of the first floor of the Farm House into an office and reporting room. The old office in the front room on the west side was refurbished as a parlor for the boarders. The bookcases, said to have room for 2,000 books, were probably moved to the east rooms at this time. Roberts hoped that the trustees would approve extending gas lighting from the Main Building to the Farm House but they rejected the idea. Kerosene lamps continued to furnish the lighting at the Farm House for some time. The only significant improvement funded by the trustees was $200 in much needed furniture for the Farm House.

The Roberts's dream of returning to their home in Mount Pleasant slowly faded away. Roberts renewed his contract with the college for 1872 and 1873. He received a pay increase of $400 and a new title, professor of practical agriculture. Mrs. Roberts asked the trustees to consider hiring someone else to look after the house and boarders. Her first request was either ignored or turned down. In 1872 she made a similar request. After this second request, a special committee from the trustees met with her and Mr. Roberts and apparently succeeded in convincing her to continue as housekeeper. It was probably a matter of economics as well as of housing.

It was the spring of 1873 when Roberts's eyes began to bother him. He blamed it on overwork and reading in the dim light at the Farm House. Roberts said it was his wife's concern for his health that prompted him to resign, but the trustees' constant disagreements and wrangling were probably a contributing factor. Roberts handed the trustees his resignation in the fall of 1873 and asked to be relieved of his responsibilities by the end of December. His resignation shocked the trustees. They tried unsuccessfully to keep Roberts at the college, even re-electing him secretary of the board for the coming year. Roberts turned them down on several occasions before the board reluctantly accepted his resignation at their November 1873 meeting. He was not planning to return to his Mount Pleasant farm but instead had applied for a teaching position at Cornell University in Ithaca, New York. In 1875 Dr. Welch recommended that the college award Roberts a master's degree in agriculture. Welch said he believed Roberts would need the academic credentials in the eastern school. After leaving Iowa, Roberts taught at Cornell University for 30 years and retired as a professor emeritus.

The college slowly changed during the three years Roberts managed the farm. Several new buildings were completed: a horse barn east of the Farm House, a mechanic workshop, a workshop on the west campus, and an addition to the Main Building which added much-needed dormitory space. In 1873 there were three faculty houses plus the Farm House and 17 faculty members and their families on campus. There also were 273 students. Dr. Foote moved from the Farm House in 1872 and shared one of the houses with Dr. Alexander Thomson. Those faculty members who did not live in one of the campus houses boarded in the Main Building or the Farm House. Some of the local farm families also took in boarders from the college. The small but growing town of Ames was still too far away to really provide convenient housing for the college although local businessmen D. A. Bigelow and H. C. Huntington promoted Ames as only a fifteen-minute walk from the State Agricultural College.

Millikan Stalker.
Courtesy of Iowa State University Library/University Archives

Almost immediately after Roberts's resignation arrangements were made for his replacement. Millikan Stalker, one of Roberts's former students and a November graduate of the college, accepted the position as superintendent of the college farm and instructor in agriculture. Stalker was neither a young nor an inexperienced college graduate. He was a mature, 32-year-old who had taught school in Springdale, Iowa, before returning to college to complete a degree. Stalker received the same benefits as Roberts—a salary and room and board at the Farm House. He also inherited the housekeeping problem at the Farm House. Stalker was a bachelor with no wife to take over the housekeeping duties that Mrs. Roberts had supervised. Even Mrs. Thomson, the college cook, turned down the job, which offered a salary of $250 a year plus room and board. In desperation, Millikan turned to his younger sister, Sallie, who like himself had just graduated from the college in November. Sallie was living at Dr. Jones's house and worked for him in the college treasurer's office. Her fiancé was attending medical school in Philadelphia and they didn't plan to marry until he graduated and set up practice. To Millikan's great relief, Sallie accepted the housekeeper's position at the Farm House, where they moved after the Roberts family left at the beginning of January 1874.

Millikan Stalker began his new job in the midst of a scandal at the college that had developed over the mismanagement of bonds. Local Ames residents, headed by Colonel Lucian Quincy Hoggatt, the newly elected state representative of Story County, demanded an explanation from the trustees. At a marathon public meeting attended by the members of the community and the state legislature, the trustees defended the college against any misconduct. The charges were never proven but Colonel Hoggatt continued to keep a close eye on the college activities. It wasn't just a question of mismanagement of funds; Colonel Hoggatt was among a growing number of Story and Boone county residents who believed the college was expanding its curriculum beyond the original intent and should get back to the basics proposed by the founders of the college. Their interest was sincere. They had put their own time and money into the college and were truly concerned that it not stray from the path of agricultural studies. After the flare-up with the community, the legislature took a drastic step and removed all 15 members of the board of trustees of the college and reestablished it as a five-member board.

Sallie Stalker Smith.
Reminiscences of Iowa Agricultural College, 1897

At the May 1874 meeting of the trustees, Millikan Stalker asked the board to hire Sallie as his assistant so she could take over his duties as secretary of the board. Sallie received $100 a year as assistant secretary for the board, which delighted Millikan and freed up his time to supervise the farm and prepare his classroom lectures. Millikan also was given permission to conduct any experiments on the farm that he could afford within the resources he had. His first project was a comparison of various ways of growing and preparing corn for feed and its effect on the farm animals.

Sallie Stalker was a talented, hardworking woman with abilities far beyond those required of a housekeeper. But in the 1870s the matron of the Farm House was not just a housekeeper. She kept up the garden; she managed a domestic staff which did the cooking and cleaning; and she ordered all the supplies for the house, including new dishes, tables, chairs, and carpeting. She did all this and was a gracious hostess to the boarders and trustees who continued to expect a room and hot meals at the Farm House when they met at the college. Sallie managed the money at the Farm House and collected $4.00 a week for room and meals from the regular boarders. The trustees, while on college business, received free room and meals and anyone else could buy a single meal at the Farm House for 50 cents.

Millikan Stalker soon developed a reputation as a very generous person and often put his own money into his college work. When the college couldn't afford another barn, Millikan paid to have it built. Millikan's outstanding work resulted in the renewal of his contract for 1875 and a pay increase to $1,200 a year. As matron of the Farm House and assistant secretary of the trustees, Sallie also received a raise to $500 a year with room and board.

The trustees were surprised when Sallie asked for a leave of absence from her duties during the 1874-75 winter vacation. She had planned for sometime to attend medical school but waited to tell the trustees until she was accepted for the winter term and approved for a scholarship at Women's Medical College in Philadelphia. Sallie's choice of school was motivated by her fiancé, Irving W. Smith, an 1872 graduate of Iowa State Agricultural College, who was attending medical school at Jefferson Medical College near the Women's Medical College in Philadelphia.

Professor Stanton took over Sallie's duties as secretary of the board until she returned in May 1875. (Sallie was enrolled during the 1874-75 school year and attended the fall and winter sessions. Some references indicate she attended medical school for two years but the official records indicate that it was two semester sessions—the fall of 1874 and the spring of 1875.) Exactly who took over as housekeeper during Sallie's leave isn't clear but she may have left sufficient orders for the staff to continue during her absence. Most of the faculty left the college during the winter break, leaving only the farmhands at the house. This probably was why the trustees granted Sallie's request. What kind of service the trustees received when they met in January 1875 at the Farm House is anyone's guess.

Sallie Stalker returned to the college in the summer of 1875 but waited until later in the year to announce her wedding plans and her resignation from the Farm House position. Her fiancé, Dr. Smith, set up practice in Charles City, Iowa, after his graduation in 1875 and was eagerly waiting for Sallie to join him. Sallie's last official day at the Farm House was March 1, 1876. After their marriage, the Smiths worked and lived in Charles City until 1893, when Dr. Smith returned to Iowa State Agricultural College as professor of pathology and therapeutics and as the college physician. When Dr. Smith died in 1895, Sallie again accepted a position at the college and later moved back in with Millikan, who then lived in Dr. Welch's former home on campus.

The trustees were more fortunate in finding a replacement for Sallie than they had been in replacing Mrs. Roberts. Millikan Stalker's position as superintendent of the farm and professor at the college continued to provide him with room and board at the Farm House but he was still a bachelor and not in a position to look after the management of the house as his sister had. Sallie gave the trustees her resignation in January, so they had time to advertise for a replacement before she left. The trustees selected Mrs. Ellen (Ella) Milligan, a 39-year-old widow from Ottumwa, Iowa, over all the applicants. Mrs. Milligan had two sons who were finishing high school and the position at the college provided her with an income and housing for the family. Her younger son, Harry, enrolled in the military tactics courses at the college for the 1876 spring term when Mrs. Milligan began her job at the Farm House. William Milligan also attended classes at the college, but neither boy graduated.

As the college increased in size and complexity the trustees began to delegate more of the daily responsibilities to the various departments of the college. Mrs. Milligan was given complete charge of the Farm House. She made the decisions on purchasing supplies for the house as long as she kept within the budget and presented a monthly report to the college treasurer's office. The three-acre farm garden was transferred to the Farm House boarding department, which she managed. It was cultivated and planted with nursery stock of her choosing. The boarding fees at the Farm House were increased

from $4.00 to $5.00 a week for the months of November through
March because of the rising costs of wood for the heating stoves, and
to $4.50 a week the rest of the year. The farmhands paid a special
year-round rate of $3.50 a week.

At a time when campus housing was scarce, it must have been
especially irritating to have the trustees order Mrs. Milligan to reserve
one bedroom in the Farm House strictly for overnight guests, an action that was probably in response to a visitor's complaint or trustees
who found themselves without a bed for the night. The addition of
rooms in the Main Building in 1871 temporarily relieved a critical
housing shortage for the students but housing the faculty continued
to plague the trustees. Of the three faculty houses built on campus,
one belonged to Dr. Welch; the other to faculty member George W.
Jones, who often boarded other faculty members; and the third was
shared by several faculty members. Rooms at the Farm House were
always full and rooms at the Main Building were at a premium. At
least one faculty member, Professor Geddes, and his family lived in
the Main Building in 1873 with over 250 students and paid $25 a
month for room and board. Campus housing for the faculty was such
an important issue that, in January 1876, the trustees turned the matter over to Dr. Welch and placed him in charge of determining who,

View of west campus, ca.
1875. *Left to right:* Dr. Jones's
house (later Dr. Geddes's),
workshop, Chemistry Building, Dr. Welch's house (*fore-
ground*), Main Building, and
Welch's barn.
*Courtesy of Iowa State University
Library/University Archives*

in the best interest of the college, should be given space in the faculty houses, the Farm House, and the Main Building. By November 1876, the Main Building was again bulging at the seams. More than one faculty member wrote angry letters protesting the housing arrangements.

To Mrs. Milligan's relief, the trustees decided to move their week-long meetings to the Main Building, freeing up space at the Farm House. It wasn't that she disliked the trustees, it was their cigar smoke she disliked. Everyone knew when the trustees were in session from the billowing clouds of smoke that surrounded them and filled the Farm House. To further relieve the crowded conditions in the house, the woodhouse attached to the northeast end of the kitchen was plastered, repaired, and used as a dining room and office for the farm laborers. Mrs. Milligan was then able to redecorate the first-floor sitting room; new wallpaper soon appeared on the walls.

Millikan Stalker's tenure as farm superintendent was cut short not because he decided to leave the college but because Dr. Welch proposed a new department at the college for veterinary studies and selected Stalker as its director. It was a position that came naturally to Stalker, whose main interest was really animal care and breeding.

The new department opened in March 1877. Stalker delivered his final report as superintendent of the farm to the trustees in December
1876, and paid special tribute to the students, who, he said, did all
the work. He also asked the trustees to carefully reconsider the superintendent's position, saying it was nearly impossible for one person to handle all the responsibilities delegated to the farm department. Apparently little had changed since former Superintendent
Thomson's days. Millikan continued to live at the Farm House when
he took over the veterinary department but since he was no longer
directly connected to the farm, he paid rent to Mrs. Milligan just like
everyone else.

        When Thomson had resigned back in 1869, the trustees had
more or less ignored his complaints, but the same concerns spoken
by Stalker several years later had the opposite effect. The trustees
took Stalker's advice. When they advertised the superintendent's position, no mention was made of teaching duties or any other service
to the college except those directly related to the farm. Of course, the
salary was adjusted to $1,200 a year plus room and board. (Stalker
had been paid $1,800 a year as superintendent and instructor.) When
no acceptable applicant surfaced, the trustees turned to Joseph Lan-
caster Budd, who had accepted a position at the college as professor
of horticulture and forestry for the 1877 spring term. The trustees
struck quite a deal with Budd. He agreed to take over the farm temporarily in addition to his teaching duties without any additional
salary. Unlike the previous superintendents, who always received free
room and board at the Farm House, Budd paid $15 a week for his
family during the summer months.
        Professor Budd, originally from New York, was 43 years old
when he accepted the position at the college. He received his early
education at the Monticello Academy in New York and in 1855 accepted a teaching position in a Galesburg, Illinois, school. In 1858, at
the age of 24, he bought a farm in Shellsburg, Benton County, Iowa,
and later established the Benton County Nursery. His marriage in
1861 to Sarah Breed, a member of a prominent eastern family, was a
happy one.
        Professor Budd managed to combine his teaching position with
that of the farm superintendent for an entire year. He seemed to have
endless energy and enthusiasm for the college. He took it upon himself to make improvements on the college grounds and farm although
it wasn't part of his regular responsibilities. He directed the con-

Budd family portrait, ca. 1882. *Left to right:* Joseph L., Allen, Etta May, and Sarah Breed Budd.
Courtesy of Iowa State University Library/University Archives

struction of embankments along Squaw Creek on the east side of the college to protect the rich bottomland from flooding and washing away and ordered repairs to the college bridges, which were rapidly deteriorating and making travel through campus perilous. When he discovered water standing in the cellar of the Farm House, he put people to work laying tiles along the foundation of the house to drain off the water. It was too late, however, to save the horticulture stock which was stored in the cellar. When the trustees turned down Budd's request for a greenhouse for his horticulture plants because they couldn't afford to build one, Budd loaned the college the money and built the greenhouse himself. The college later repaid his loan.

Joseph Budd; his wife, Sarah; and their 15-year-old daughter, Etta May; and 13-year-old son, Allen, arrived at the college in early March 1877. Mrs. Milligan was at the Farm House to greet the Budd family and to see that they were comfortably settled in. It's almost impossible to determine who was living at the Farm House when the Budd family arrived because records no longer exist from the boarding department. Some of the faculty continued to board at the Main Building, some at the Farm House or with area farmers who offered rooms in their homes. The former farm manager, A. J. Graves, offered housing in his home south of the college, as did former college tenant farmer, William Fitchpatrick, both of whom were now prosperous farmers and businessmen. Faculty could also live in the growing community of Ames but getting back and forth to the campus was always dependent on the weather. Those that did live in Ames could catch a ride on the college bus (wagon or buggy) that made the trip from the Ames railroad station to the campus several times a day if the roads were not washed out. The trustees finally agreed to pay any faculty member who could not find housing on campus an additional $200 a year towards their housing expenses and left the matter of finding housing up to the individual.

In 1877 one enterprising faculty member, Professor Pope, purchased land across from the college on what is now the west corner of Gray Street and Lincoln Way and built a two story frame house for his family. He sold it to the college in 1884. Professor Budd did not plan to make the Farm House his permanent home and he received a 10-year lease from the college on an acre of land northwest of the Farm House (on the present site of Carrie Chapman Catt Hall, the former Botany Building and before that Agriculture Hall) and began construction on his house in the summer of 1877. Like many of the houses built on campus, it was later moved to another site to make room for a larger building. In 1892 the Budd house was moved southeast of the Farm House to the site of the original Dairy Industry Building.

Mrs. Milligan completed her second year as matron at the Farm House while the search was continuing for someone to take over Budd's duties as superintendent of the farm. She was not in any jeopardy of losing her job but it must have been on her mind until the trustees finally renewed her contract for another year. Although Professor Budd was acting superintendent, Mrs. Budd did not have an official position at the Farm House as previous wives of the superintendents had. Mrs. Budd was probably delighted just to room at the Farm House and spend her time planning her new home and caring for her family.

The Budd children, Etta May and Allen, attended school with the other faculty children who lived on campus. The younger children were tutored by college students, but when it was possible the children attended classes at the college. (Although the Fitchpatrick children attended the Hoggatt School when they lived on the farm in the early 1860s, the Ames school was no longer just a walk across the field. It was now in town, which was a long way from the college.) Etta May and Allen later graduated from the college and Allen re-

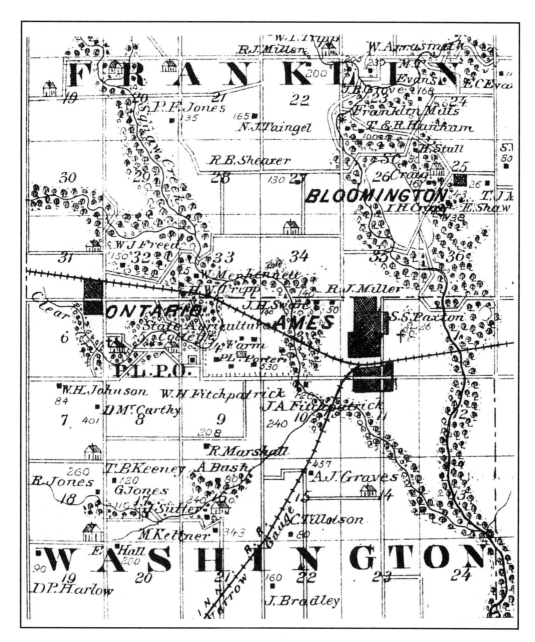

Map of Washington Township showing Ames, college farm, and land
owned by Graves and Fitchpatrick families, ca. 1875.
Story County Atlas. *Courtesy of the Ames Public Library*

turned to farm in Shellsburg. Etta May began teaching art at Iowa
State and later joined the faculty at Simpson College before returning
to Ames some years later. It was while Etta May taught art classes at
Simpson College that she met George Washington Carver and played
a significant role in convincing him to pursue a science career at Iowa
State Agricultural College.

In November 1877, the trustees hired H. H. Robinson to take
over the college farm as of March 1, 1878. Professor Budd received
an additional $200 for his past year's work as the superintendent and
agreed to remain as an adviser until Robinson could become familiar
with the farm activities. It isn't clear why Robinson was only offered
$1,000 instead of the $1,200 salary advertised the year before, but it
might have had to do with the matron's position. What is clear, however, is Robinson's dissatisfaction with his position at the college from
the very beginning. When the trustees hired Robinson they authorized him to buy dairy cows for the college herds and asked him to
make the selection as soon as possible. When Robinson stopped at
the college in January to survey the livestock needs, he stayed at the
Farm House and was annoyed that he was asked to pay for his room
and board. He spent 15 days in January and February buying cattle
and each time he returned to the college farm he was asked to pay
room and board for himself and his two helpers. Robinson felt this
was a deliberate slight and that he should have been extended room
and board as a courtesy since he was on official college business.
When Robinson arrived at the college farm in March, this time as the
superintendent, it was Mrs. Milligan's unpleasant duty to tell him that
only one sleeping room was reserved at the Farm House for his family. He became angry because he believed the trustees promised him
a house for his family. He wrote the trustees asking for an additional
$4.00 a week for his family's expenses which they agreed to pay him
as long as he was employed at the college. It isn't known whether or
not Robinson eventually found rooms for his family or if the family
simply returned to their own home, which was close enough to the
college for Robinson to have made frequent trips back to visit.

In November 1878, Robinson's absences from the farm came to
the attention of Dr. Welch, who became so concerned about the farm
that he hired Harry Adair to look after the livestock. Adair received
$30 a month plus board and laundry at the Farm House. This arrange-
ment lasted only a month because the trustees refused to pay any
money for an assistant for Robinson. The trustees had already de-

cided not to renew Mr. Robinson's contract for another year. They did insist that he complete his year's contract and be on the farm every day or his salary would be withheld. It was up to John N. Dixon, one of the trustees, to negotiate a settlement with Robinson for the termination of his employment contract.

The decision not to renew Robinson's contract had an immediate effect on Mrs. Milligan. The trustees voted to elect the Honorable John C. Hiatt, a farmer, livestock dealer, and former legislator from Lynnville, Iowa, as superintendent of the farm for the coming year. Hiatt's wife, Esther, requested that she be allowed to take over the housekeeper's duties at the Farm House so she and the children could live with her husband on the college farm. This meant that Mrs. Milligan's contract was not renewed for 1879. The trustees assured her that her work was entirely satisfactory and the only reason she was asked to retire was to make room for the superintendent and his wife. Mrs. Milligan requested that the trustees put their assurance in writing (she may have wanted this document for an employment reference). The trustees also gave Mrs. Milligan $25 to compensate her for the use of her furniture at the Farm House. She returned to Ottumwa, Iowa, where she lived with a sister until her death on July 3, 1911, at the age of 73. Her oldest son, William, continued to attend Iowa State College until 1880, when he returned to Ottumwa and took a position as a salesman for J. H. Merrill & Co. His younger brother, Harry, a freshman in 1879 according to Minnie Knapp Mayo, married in 1880 and later moved to Lake Charles, Louisiana, a growing community of former Iowans with Iowa Agricultural College connections.

John C. Hiatt's career as superintendent began during a year of transition for the college farm. Dr. Welch was in the process of developing a new faculty position of practical and experimental agriculture which would essentially replace the farm superintendent's job. Perhaps Hiatt was aware of this when he signed his one-year contract, which began in March 1879. Before he arrived on campus, the trustees appointed him to a committee with Dr. Welch and Dr. Budd to investigate the possibility of developing a creamery on the college campus, an endeavor that would cause a great deal of resentment among the businessmen of Ames. It would be an exciting year for Hiatt.

John Hiatt and his wife, Esther, were originally from Indiana. After their marriage in 1866, they moved to Iowa to be near his family.

The Hiatts had two children, a son Willie and an adopted daughter, Luella Bufkin, whom they had raised from infancy. Hiatt was a successful farmer, stock dealer, member of the County Board of Supervisors, and former Representative from the 17th District in Jasper County. The family owned a 300-acre farm in Lynnville, Iowa, which Hiatt rented out when he took the job at the college.

The Hiatts were allowed to run the Farm House boarding department as a separate department from the college and could charge boarders whatever they felt necessary to cover their expenses with one exception: they could only charge the farmhands $3.00 a week for room and board. When Mrs. Milligan managed the Farm House she was responsible to the college treasurer's office for the money she collected and spent but the Hiatts were not required to make any financial reports to the college. They were, however, required to inventory all the furniture in the house belonging to the college and were responsible for its use and care. (There are no surviving furniture inventories.) The previous year Mrs. Milligan had spent almost $300 for new furniture and the trustees were not about to purchase any more furniture for the Hiatts or the Farm House. The vegetable garden planted by Mrs. Milligan was at Mrs. Hiatt's disposal for the Farm House kitchen, and they were allowed all the wood they could use from the timber on the farm as long as they paid a driver to collect the wood for them. They received a joint salary of $1,500 a year and free room and board at the Farm House for themselves and their two children. President Welch also made it clear to the Hiatts that no students could board at the Farm House without his express permission. Perhaps Dr. Welch believed the Farm House lacked the strict supervision of the students' activities which he maintained in the Main Building or that only the more mature, older students could survive in the less formal atmosphere at the Farm House.

Hiatt's first charge from the trustees was to visit other creameries and get ideas of what would be needed to start a creamery at the college. The trustees allocated $500 for equipment and another $1,200 for dairy cattle, which Mr. Hiatt was to select. They originally suggested that the office and wood house connected to the Farm House would be suitable for the creamery, but Professor Budd and Dr. Welch thought otherwise. The creamery began operation in the summer of 1879 in a small, new building southeast of the Farm House. The creamery supplied the college with milk and cheese and later gained a reputation for some of the best ice cream sold anywhere. The Ames dairy merchants saw this as unfair competition and began an unsuccessful campaign to close the college creamery.

Hiatt's success on the farm was hampered by a severe drought during the hot summer of 1879. The student newspaper, the *Aurora,* gave Superintendent Hiatt high marks for keeping the farm in good condition despite the weather. "Everything," they wrote, "looks neat and in order, oats, rye, wheat, hay. Corn crop suffering from extreme drought." The newspaper also ran a notice of a liberal reward offered by the farm superintendent for the return of "the six chickens so carefully fed up for the State Fair."

At the July 1879 meeting of the trustees, Dr. Welch presented his plan for a new Department of Practical and Experimental Agriculture. The trustees approved the department and Dr. Welch's selection of Seaman Knapp as head of the department. Knapp would begin his career at the college on March 1, 1880, and would take over the responsibility of the college farm from Hiatt.

When the college opened its doors in 1869, no one imagined how successful the college would be in attracting students to this rather unorthodox school. Nor could they have imagined the competition that would develop for housing, which later forced the trustees to turn away potential students. The Farm House became a thriving boarding department at the college, offering shelter to practically every new faculty member and serving as the first home on the campus to college President Welch and his family. As the college farm evolved from its modest beginnings into the Department of Practical and Experimental Agriculture, the Farm House would become the home of another president of the college, Seaman Knapp.

5 · The Knapp Years: Sketches of Nineteenth-Century College Life

*A*dvocates of Seaman Knapp's appointment as head of the new Department of Practical and Experimental Agriculture at the college believed, as biographer Joseph Bailey wrote, that Knapp was about to "work some minor miracles for the farmers of the state,…advancing an…expanded program of farm experimentation at the college farm." It was a subject, Bailey noted, that Knapp frequently wrote about in the *Farmer's Journal*. President Welch had the utmost faith in Knapp. But Knapp became frustrated by the state legislature's lack of interest in funding the college and went after federal money for his programs. While living at the Farm House, he began to draft a bill that was the basis for the Hatch Experiment Station Act passed by Congress in 1887. Unfortunately, Knapp's dream of having an experiment station at the agriculture college became a reality only after he was no longer connected with the college.

It was by way of an accident that Seaman Knapp actually came to Iowa—an accident that left him crippled and on crutches for nearly seven years and completely changed his life. He had trained to be a teacher and minister and was in the midst of opening a new school in Poultney, Vermont, when he fell and injured his knee. Soon he was unable to walk without crutches. When his health did not improve after a year, his physician advocated that Knapp get out into the air and away from the pulpit. He moved his family to eastern Iowa where the farmland was fertile and inexpensive. He soon found manual labor on the farm too strenuous and accepted positions as head of the Iowa Institute for the Blind in Vinton, Iowa, and pastor of the Methodist Episcopal Church. Never one to have a limited field of interest, he also became a banker and a livestock breeder. To promote his livestock business he would lecture to anyone who would listen to him about the benefits of purebred livestock and wrote numerous articles on scientific farming including a series of articles titled "Talks on

Pigs" for the *Farmer's Journal.* As a banker in Vinton, Iowa, he helped farmers get low interest loans and encouraged the agricultural settlement of his county. He was president of the Stock Breeders Association of Iowa, which, according to Joseph Bailey, attracted members such as "Uncle Henry" Wallace; A. S. Welch, president of the Iowa State Agricultural College; and "Tama Jim" Wilson, a future faculty member of the college. It was through his association with the Stock Breeders Association that Dr. Welch became acquainted with Knapp.

Seaman Knapp and his wife, Maria, both came from farm backgrounds and met as students at Troy Conference Academy in Vermont when they were 16. Both graduated from Troy Academy and Seaman continued his schooling at Union College in New York, graduating Phi Beta Kappa with a bachelor of arts degree. He and Maria were married on August 6, 1856, and both accepted teaching positions at the Washington County Seminary and Collegiate Institute in Fort Edward, New York. Neither Knapp nor his wife had any idea that they would one day find themselves in Iowa.

Seaman Knapp was hired as professor of practical and experimental agriculture on March 1, 1880. His duties were to include supervising the college farm and managing the college boarding department. He was to receive a salary of $1,600 a year and housing for his family at the Farm House. Mrs. Knapp would be permitted to continue running a boarding department at the house but Dr. Welch cautioned her not to board any students without his approval. The trustees also gave Dr. Knapp permission to board his horse on the farm but said he could keep his family's cow there only if he paid for its feed.

In late February 1880, the Knapp family arrived at the Ames railroad station and began the final leg of their trip to the college. Herman Knapp, Seaman's 16-year-old son, later told historian Gladys Meade that it was the coldest winter morning he could ever remember. He was in charge of the freight car loaded with household possessions, the Berkshire hogs Seaman was bringing to the college, and the family's horse. Herman said he "hopped out of the freight car,...mounted the animal [horse] and rode off to the college...to get the workmen at the Farm House and start them down with wagons to unload the goods." He also said it was only the warmth of the bareback horse that kept him from freezing to death that day.

The Knapps arrived at the Farm House before most of the boarders returned from winter break. The former superintendent and his wife, Mr. and Mrs. Hiatt, left everything in good order but the trustees requested that the Knapps take a complete inventory of the

Seaman Knapp.
Courtesy of Iowa State University Library/University Archives

Maria Knapp.
Courtesy of Iowa State University Library/University Archives

Herman Knapp.
Courtesy of Iowa State University Library/University Archives

furniture in the house before they settled in with their own belongings. They spent several days opening boxes, assigning bedrooms for the family, and just generally getting acquainted with their new home. It was easy to see that the house had received hard use during its 20 years. The wooden floors were scuffed and the woodwork was chipped. They were surprised at the number of bedrooms in the house—eight on the top two floors. Even more surprising were the large closets in six of the bedrooms. Instead of the typical kerosene lamps, the Farm House now had gas lighting which had been extended from the Main Building after Mr. Roberts left the farm in 1873. Kerosene lamps were still used, however, because not everyone trusted gas.

The two older Knapp children, 16-year-old Herman and 18-year-old Minnie, enrolled in spring classes at the college. Herman found work on the farm and Minnie worked in the Main Building office. The two younger boys, seven-year-old Arthur and nine-year-old Bradford, attended school with the other campus children. After school they did their share of work on the farm. The youngest of the children, two-year-old Helen, stayed by her mother's side while she worked on the housekeeping schedules and planned meals for a mixed company of up to 30 people for dinner, including the trustees when they met at the college.

Knapp began teaching classes within a few weeks of his arrival on campus. He also spent considerable time during that first spring and summer working with Professors Budd and Beal making improvements to the Squaw Creek channel in an effort to prevent the constant flooding of the college farm's pasture and fields. (They would not be surprised to know that the flooding problem continues over 100 years later.) Dr. Welch also assigned Knapp the job of assisting Professor Budd with the design and building of boarding cottages to alleviate the cramped quarters in the Main Building. In 1879 a group of enterprising young students received permission to build a house, which they named Fair Oak Mansion, on a site suggested to be the present west edge of the Molecular Biology Building on Pammel Drive. Even with the addition of Fair Oak, the lack of housing continued to force the college to turn away prospective students.

At the end of Seaman Knapp's first year at the college, the trustees renewed his contract and paid him an additional $200 a year for supervising the farm work but canceled his right to keep a cow on the farm. As a matter of fact, the trustees refused to allow any faculty member to keep a cow on campus—not even the president—because it was causing problems with the farm operations. Probably for reasons of economy, the trustees also told Maria Knapp that she would have to begin paying for the vegetables she used from the farm garden. It would be another year before the trustees agreed to give Mrs. Knapp $45 to buy a new stove for the kitchen, which she and Mrs. Welch purchased with Dr. Welch's advice. Perhaps to make up for the loss of the free vegetables, or to reward her for her generosity in having donated some of her own firewood to the creamery and the workmen, the trustees agreed to let Maria have all the "fallen wood" she could find on the farm without charge, as long as she had it hauled to the Farm House and cut at her own expense.

In the spring of 1881, Knapp convinced the trustees to make some repairs to the Farm House. He replaced missing shingles on the south side of the roof where water had damaged the ceiling and walls on the third floor. On the first floor, the kitchen drain was cleaned and repaired and floorboards were repaired in the east office room. On the exterior of the house, water-damaged caps above the windows and doors were repaired or replaced. The following spring, on April 8, 1882, a devastating cyclone hit the college, damaging roofs, crumbling chimneys, and turning over a college bus, which injured several people. Professor Budd's house, just northwest of the Farm House, lost a chimney. Miraculously the Farm House was spared and the newly reshingled roof remained intact. The devastation from the cyclone was so extensive that spring planting took a back seat to campus cleanup. The entire campus and farm were covered with up-rooted trees and fallen branches. The horticulture barn was destroyed and the walls on Dr. Welch's home were severely damaged. It took the entire spring to pick up the debris caused by the violent cyclone.

It was during 1882—Dr. Knapp's second year at the college—that Dr. Welch accepted an invitation from the federal agricultural commission to inspect the agricultural schools of Europe on its behalf. For some time the trustees and Dr. Welch had been at odds over what Earle D. Ross later wrote was "an old argument between the scientists and the vocationalists." Probably to give everyone a little time to reflect on the causes of a growing rift between them, the trustees

The Knapp family in front of the Farm House, ca. 1885. *Left to right:* Mrs. Maria Knapp, Helen Louise, Arthur, Seaman, Minnie, Herman, and Bradford.
Farm House Museum Archives

granted Dr. Welch's request for a leave of absence from September 1, 1882, until March 1883. In November 1882, the trustees placed Seaman Knapp in charge of the college as vice-president while Welch was in Europe. Knapp's salary was raised to $2,000 a year. Knapp, however, made it clear to the trustees that he supported Dr. Welch and planned to turn the job back to Welch upon his return. Welch's absence actually consolidated the resolve of the trustees to replace him as president of the college.

While Welch was in Europe, the trustees authorized Knapp to travel to Washington, D.C., to attend an agricultural convention to lobby for the establishment of state experiment stations. Dr. Knapp's attempt to do experiments on the college farm were thwarted from the day he arrived on campus because of a lack of money. At times, he and other faculty members put their own money into their re search and equipment. He couldn't understand the state legislature's lack of interest in funding the experimental work being done at the college and he directed his attention instead to a proposal for federal money to support his research and demonstration plots. Early in 1882, Knapp spoke to the Stock Breeders Association and presented the first draft of legislation he and Professor Charles Bessey prepared for a federal program of experiment stations. The idea wasn't new; Dr. Welch had attended meetings where it was first proposed more than 10 years earlier, but it was Knapp and Bessey who drew up the proposal for legislation that was presented to Congress in May 1882. It was, however, soundly defeated. As a result Knapp found himself traveling to Washington in January 1883, during the college's winter break, to again lobby for support for federally funded experiment stations. The bill was reintroduced in 1883 after Knapp's trip to Washington and was again defeated. It would be four years later, in 1887, before the legislation was rewritten and enacted as the Hatch Experiment Station Act.

It's difficult to know or describe the emotional effects on the Knapp family from the turmoil taking place at the college during 1883. Welch returned from Europe to find a hostile Board of Trustees. Dr. Knapp found himself between his old and dear friend, Dr. Welch, and the trustees. It's certain the Farm House was the scene of wrenching family discussions and meals laced with conversation about Dr. Welch and his dismissal from the presidency of the college. The Knapp and Welch families were close friends, and it must have been particularly difficult for Mary Welch and Maria Knapp as they witnessed the strain on their husbands' relationship.

In November 1883, as Joseph Bailey described the scene in his biography of Seaman Knapp, the trustees "unceremoniously…ousted [Welch] the man chiefly responsible for organizing and guiding during its first fourteen years the college over which the Board again ruled with capricious irresponsibility." Dr. Welch's removal as president of the college caused a major uproar on campus and in the nearby town of Ames. The leading citizens of Ames signed a petition against Dr. Welch's removal and the students at the college added their support. The trustees, however, ignored the petition and on November 27, 1883, removed Welch from the presidency of the college and immediately elected Seaman Knapp to take his place as of December 1, 1883. In accepting the one-year term as president of the college, Knapp also retained his position as professor of practical and experimental agriculture and continued to supervise the college farm. The trustees reduced Welch to the rank of professor but agreed to pay his salary as president for the remainder of the year. Dr. Welch was a man of incredible strength and determination. He remained at the college as a professor of history and philosophy and when called upon occasionally took charge of the farm until his death in 1889.

In the same month that Seaman Knapp became president of the college, his two oldest children, Herman and Minnie, graduated with the college's 12th graduating class. Herman accepted a position at the college as deputy to the treasurer and agreed to lecture in agriculture for the coming spring session for which he would receive a total yearly salary of $500. Herman and Minnie continued to live at the Farm House after graduation and Herman helped his father on the farm when he could. Minnie assisted her mother at home. What should have been a joyous time for the Knapps was marred by the controversy surrounding the manner in which the trustees ousted Dr. Welch and placed Dr. Knapp in charge of the college.

There is no record of any major improvements being made to the Farm House during 1884, the year it was the president's home. Certainly the social activity for the faculty focused on the Farm House, but it was still a boarding house. Maria Knapp took on the added responsibility of the president's wife with confidence and refinement. According to college faculty member D. E. W. Stanton, Maria was "gracious, tactful, tender,…instinctively knew the right word to use, the right advice to offer, and always, the particular way in which the strength needed could be given. Mrs. Knapp was not only a woman of culture but she used her intellectual attainments in a way to command the respect and honor of all her associates."

Map of central campus, 1884. Published by the *Daily Republican,* Cedar
Rapids, Iowa, 1884.
Courtesy of Iowa State University Library/University Archives

It may seem strange to us that the college president's family
shared its home with boarders or that the president's wife was expected to manage the boarding department in her own home. But it
was a time at the college when everyone, including the president and
his wife, was expected to handle a variety of responsibilities. This
sharing of duties caused some minor conflicts but generally drew the
families together. The campus had a community of its own, which
tended to insulate the college from the town.

During Knapp's year as president of the college he abolished
the mandatory work requirement for students, which he said was a
dismal failure. He supported the decision to grant the Edison Electric
Light Company a commission to build a plant on campus that would
generate enough electricity to light the campus with 250 incandes-
cent lamps. He witnessed the completion of the Sanitary Building
(hospital) and the Veterinary Hospital on campus. The most impor-

tant event during his year as president was a significant change in the Iowa legislature's interpretation of the Morrill Act, the main source of financial support for land-grant colleges. Senator Preston M. Sutton of Marshalltown, Iowa, had long contended that Senator Morrill did not mean to restrict the land-grant colleges from teaching literature and the social sciences. With Senator Morrill's support, the Iowa legislature redefined the Iowa law establishing the land-grant college and expanded its academic curriculum to include "such other branches of learning as will most practically and liberally educate the agriculture and industrial classes in the several pursuits and professions of life." While it did not immediately effect Dr. Knapp, the impact of this change would be debated long into the 20th century.

At the end of Knapp's year as president, he asked for a leave of absence from the college. He had not taken a vacation in his five years of service to the college and planned to spend a month with his family in the sunny state of Louisiana. He did not tell the trustees he was considering looking for employment elsewhere. The strain of working with a Board of Trustees which seemed determined to interfere with the daily management of the college probably contributed to his decision. The trustees granted Seaman's request for a vacation and appointed him professor of agriculture and superintendent of the farm for the coming year, 1885. They also elected Professor J. L. Budd as president pro tem until they could select a new president for the college.

While Seaman Knapp took the family to Louisiana, Herman Knapp stayed at the Farm House and took charge of the farm during his father's absence. Herman was now an assistant professor of agriculture in addition to his job as assistant to the treasurer and received a salary of $650 a year. He was also engaged to be married in the fall to a fellow classmate, Mary McDonald, and he was in the midst of looking for a more lucrative position which would support a wife and family.

When Seaman Knapp returned to the college for the 1885 spring session, he had already decided to accept a position in Louisiana at a considerably higher salary than he received as president of the Iowa college. It wasn't just the salary that interested him, it was the opportunity to continue his research and help encourage farmers to settle in Lake Charles, Louisiana, that captured his imagination. Before he told the trustees of his plans, he agreed to represent the college at a convention of agricultural colleges and experiment stations in Washington, D.C., on July 8, 1885. His presence at this convention and the support he received from those attending would be instrumental in passage of the Hatch Experiment Station Act, but that would not happen until 1887 after Knapp had left the college.

Knapp must not have been certain his Louisiana venture would be permanent since he only asked for a one-year leave of absence for 1886 with the understanding that he would return to teach the summer session. He also recommended that Herman be given his position at the college. In the meantime, Herman had accepted a position at Dakota Agricultural College beginning in the fall of 1885. Because the trustees valued the Knapps and did not wish to lose either of them, Seaman was granted his year's leave from the college and Herman was offered and accepted the trustees' offer to remain at the college with a substantial raise. Later he took over as supervisor of the farm.

On November 26, 1885, before an admiring family, Herman Knapp married Mary W. McDonald at her parents' home in Mount Pleasant, Iowa. Mary and Herman had graduated from Iowa Agricultural College in 1883 and both seemed to be happy at the prospect of remaining in Iowa. After a brief honeymoon, Herman and Mary moved into the Farm House. The rest of the Knapp family packed their belongings and traveled by train to St. Charles, Louisiana, which would eventually become a permanent home to the Knapp family. Minnie Knapp accepted a teaching position near the family home in St. Charles and was married the following year.

Herman and Mary Knapp began their married life at the Farm House in January 1886. Mary thought she knew how cold the Farm House could be during the winters but was truly unprepared for the bitter cold. She later wrote in her diary, "It [1929] is the coldest and snowiest January since January, 1886. Herman and I lived in the Farm House that winter...our first year of wedded life....Used only such rooms as we needed, lived entirely downstairs. House heated with stoves. We didn't know it was colder than usual." Mary Knapp also wrote that Mrs. Budd said she would never spend another winter on the campus because it was so cold and, according to Mary, she never did. When the weather warmed and the college opened, Mary found work at the college as a preceptress. She received $25 for her service during the spring term.

It is not clear whether Mary took over Maria Knapp's role at the

Farm House or how many boarders were living there during the spring of 1886. It is certain that sometime during the year, probably before the end of summer, two rooms were added to the Farm House to create a duplex. There is some thought that the one-story work-men's room attached to the north end of the kitchen wood house was moved to the northeast side of the main house to form the addition. The fifth chimney also may have been added to the house at this time to provide an outlet for a stove. The addition of an east kitchen and dining area allowed the creation of a duplex with the central hallway as a dividing line. To retain privacy and separation, it is possible that, at that time, the east exterior door on the original kitchen did not open directly into the new addition as it did later.

Herman and Mary lived through these renovations at the Farm House and were there when Seaman Knapp returned for the summer session in 1886. By this time Seaman had made the final decision to remain in Louisiana and offered his resignation to the trustees. He spoke to the recently elected president of the college, William Chamberlain, about his son and recommended Herman be given a perma-nent faculty position. President Chamberlain's address to the trustees included a recommendation in favor of Herman Knapp. Chamberlain asked the trustees to "look at possibly keeping him [Herman] on even though he was young [age 22]....He took charge of the farm and showed energy, fidelity and earnestness." Chamberlain also recom-mended that Herman be paid $1,200 a year as assistant professor of agriculture and the "west half of the Farm House be granted him in view of his vacation work in charge of the farm." It wasn't until No-vember 1886 that the east half of the Farm House was mentioned in the trustees' minutes. It is possible that the east half of the Farm House, at least on the first floor, was vacant because at that time Pres-ident Chamberlain recommended it be made available to Professor Wynn's successor or to Professor Hainer "in lieu of $200 allowed for house rent." It is also not clear if either Professor Wynn or Professor Hainer actually lived in the Farm House, but the east half of the house was finally assigned to Professor A. C. Barrows, who joined the faculty in the spring of 1887. Barrows would have something to say about this arrangement before he moved his family to the college.

Meanwhile the death of General James L. Geddes left the col-lege without a treasurer and the trustees offered the position to Her-man Knapp. In February 1887, Herman Knapp became the college treasurer, recorder and manager of the book department, and the col-lege land agent. Herman began dividing his time between the office at the college and an office in Ames for the land agent. It was a fortunate opportunity for Herman and the beginning of a lifelong career at the college. Dr. Welch stepped in and took over the supervision of the farm, allowing Herman to begin his work as treasurer before his replacement on the farm could be hired.

When Herman accepted the new position at the college, he also relinquished his right to housing in the Farm House. He and Mary spent the spring of 1887 making arrangements to move across campus to Professor Stanton's home, where they lived until their own home was built. Herman received a 10-year lease on an acre of land owned by the college on the east side of the main road (Knoll Road) into campus. It was almost directly across from the future location of the Knoll, the home built for the college president in 1900. Construction began on the Knapps's home in 1888. By the time they moved into their new home, they were parents of a baby boy, Seaman Knapp II, who was born December 16, 1888.

While Herman Knapp was busy beginning his new job as treasurer of the college, Professor A. C. Barrows was struggling with his housing arrangements at the college. Barrows was given the east half of the Farm House for his family, but when he arrived at the college

View of Knoll Road going north to the Farm House, ca. 1909.
Courtesy of Iowa State University Library/University Archives

in March 1887 and looked at the space, he was instantly distressed. He wrote the trustees a passionate letter on May 23, 1887, outlining his family's predicament:

> That until it shall be in your power to offer me a permanent home, my salary may be paid me, as it has hitherto been, wholly in cash and that I be left to provide a home for myself—in explanation of the above, I accepted my professorship with the understanding that I should take a house on account of salary....I was informed of the place to put a half of the Farm House in order for me but I declined to agree to take it till I should have a chance to examine its accommodations. That chance I now have and Mrs. Barrows and myself are agreed that for us, with our large family, life in this house would be uncomfortable and exhausting to an extent that it would interfere with my work. It would be better if the worst should happen, that I should toil on in loneliness here with my family comfortably housed, than that we should all be here in an uncomfortable house.

President Chamberlain insisted that Barrows be given South Hall, Welch's former home on campus, for his family. Instead the trustees assigned the west nine rooms of the Farm House to Barrows at their May 26, 1887, meeting and instructed that the repairs to this portion of the house be completed before Barrows moved his family to the campus. Exactly what repairs were made is uncertain, but Herman and Mary must have spent their last months at the Farm House surrounded by college carpenters getting the house in order for Professor Barrows and his family.

Allen Campbell Barrows was a former classmate and personal friend of President Chamberlain, who recommended Barrows to the trustees for the position of professor of English literature and history formerly held by Dr. Hainer. Barrows was a graduate of Phillips Academy, Andover, Massachusetts, and Western Reserve College in Cleveland, Ohio. He served in the Union army during the Civil War. After a distinguished army career he returned to academics as professor of physics and math at Western Reserve College and was later chair of the Department of English Literature and Latin. He was also a member of the County Horticultural Society and the pastor of the Con-

West side of the Farm House, with the farm office door visible on the west wall, ca. 1880s.
Courtesy of Iowa State University Library/University Archives

gregational Church in Kent, Ohio, until 1884. Chamberlain told the trustees that Barrows was the right man for the position because Barrows was, in his opinion, "in sympathy with the views of the agricultural and industrial education of Iowa State Agricultural College." Barrows was also well suited to assist Chamberlain with the required Sabbath sermons at the college, thereby saving the expense of paying someone else—a fact not lost on the trustees.

Professor Barrows was in his middle 40s when he came to the college. His first wife, Mary, died at the age of 31 in 1868, leaving him with two small sons. He remarried the following year, and one year later he and his second wife, Laura, had their first child, a daughter. The March 1887 issue of the agriculture and horticulture department's *Students' Farm Journal* noted that Barrows's family would not arrive at the college until July. There was no mention of the number of children in the family but, according to Barrows's letter to the trustees, he and his wife had a large family to house. The college newspaper later mentioned that Barrows's son Frank returned to Oberlin, Ohio, in September 1887 to continue his music studies.

While the Barrows family was getting settled in their new home at the Farm House, the trustees continued their search for someone to replace Herman Knapp as superintendent of the college farm. Ap-

parently the east side of the Farm House was reserved
for a farm superintendent and at least the first floor,
where the farm office and secretary's reporting room
still functioned, may have been vacant when the Barrows family moved into the house in the summer of
1887. With on-campus housing still at a premium it
seems likely that any bedrooms not used by the Barrows family were probably rented to the farm workers
or to Mr. Schoenleber, the farm foreman, who assisted
Dr. Welch and Herman Knapp at this time.

It was while the farm was without a superintendent and under Dr. Welch's temporary supervision that
President Chamberlain decided that it was time to
reevaluate the role of the college farm in the overall program at the college. Since the abolishment of the
mandatory student work program in 1884, most of the
work on the farm was now done by paid laborers. Al-

Allan Campbell Barrows.
*Courtesy of Iowa State Univer-
sity Library/University
Archives*

though some students still worked on the farm, their work was no
longer part of a formal program of instruction. Before making any decision about the college farm, President Chamberlain wanted to know
exactly how the college lands were being used. He requested that
Herman Knapp make a complete inventory of the land owned by the
college. Knapp's inventory showed that of the 895 acres of land included in the college campus, 465 acres were farmed or in use as pasture. One question in particular that was actively discussed by the
trustees and President Chamberlain was whether or not the college
farm should continue purely as an educational endeavor or whether
it should, as some thought, produce a profit. No definite conclusion
on the profit issue was reached but a major decision was reached
about the farmlands. Most of the land under the control of the farm
department was transferred to the horticulture department for its use.
The farm department retained control of the remaining barns, livestock, and fields.

A great deal of confusion surrounded the selection of a professor of agriculture to replace Herman Knapp. In May 1887, the trustees
elected Mr. E. M. Shelton of Kansas for the position. He was offered
a generous salary of $2,300 a year and the housing in the east half of
the Farm House for his family. Mr. Shelton was to begin work on
March 1, 1888, but after a short visit to the college in the summer of
1887, he declined the offer. In November 1887, the name of Loren

Loren Pease Smith.
Courtesy of Carl A. Kroch Library, Division of Rare and Manuscript Collections, Cornell University, Ithaca, New York

Pease Smith, a graduate of Cornell University in New York, was first mentioned by the trustees as a possibility for the position. Cornell graduates had an early connection with the Iowa Agricultural College and Smith came highly recommended. He was offered the position of professor of agriculture and complete responsibility for what remained of the college farm. On November 10, President Chamberlain ordered that no further change was to be made in the farm management until the arrival of Professor Smith. His employment contract was dated November 17, 1887, but it is not clear whether he was at the college to accept the position at that time or if he arrived at a later date. Smith was paid $1,600 a year and was given the east half of the Farm House for his living quarters. His position was guaranteed for two years by the trustees, as long as his work proved satisfactory.

As far as we know, Loren P. Smith was not married at the time he came to the college. There does not seem to be any written record concerning which rooms actually constituted the east side of the house, but we can at least be certain that the two east rooms on the first floor of the main house and probably the newly added kitchen and dining area were used by Smith. It is also possible, if he was indeed alone, that he used one of the rooms as his sleeping quarters. We do know that one of the rooms was the farm office. We know this from the trustees' fall 1888 minutes, which record the payment of $18.95 for a stove "for the room of the house occupied by him [Professor of Agriculture],...said room being used in part as farm office." All the rooms facing onto the main hallway had doors which could be closed and locked to provide privacy for Smith and the Barrows family.

There is no indication of anything but a friendly relationship between Smith and the Barrows family while they lived together in the Farm House. Students wrote about Professor Barrows in the 1894 school yearbook, the *BOMB,* saying, "If he ever feels ill-natured no one finds it out. To the students he is always a kind and obliging friend, always ready to help a student but more ready to make the student help himself." On the other hand, the students viewed Smith, who at 38 years of age looked more like a student than a professor, as one who lacked common knowledge about farming and had a superior eastern attitude. Both Professor Barrows and Smith came from classical educational backgrounds and probably found a lot in com-

mon to discuss. Smith, whose interest was science, received his undergraduate and graduate degrees from Cornell University in Ithaca,
New York, in 1872 and 1874. Although Barrows's interests were not
in the scientific area he was well known on campus (according to the
1894 yearbook) as a successful gardener whose flowers were the
envy of everyone who saw them. The student newspaper, the *Aurora,*
reported that Barrows often invited students to his home for an
"evening of spirited conversation and choice desserts prepared by his
wife Laura." Smith certainly might have joined in these gatherings at
the house.

Smith managed the college farm and taught at the college for
three years. During this time, in 1888, the state of Iowa passed legislation based on the 1887 federal Hatch Experiment Station Act, which
established an experiment station at the agricultural college. Former
trustee Robert Speer was appointed its first director. Although it was
located on the campus it was not yet a department of the college.
That would happen several years later.

Little is known of Loren P. Smith's life at the college. Earle D.

View to the northeast across the Iowa Agricultural College experiment
farm, ca. 1888. *Left:* North Hall; *right:* Professor Budd's house, which is
just west of the Farm House.
Courtesy of Iowa State University Library/University Archives

Ross wrote that Smith was "not familiar with prairie practices and seemed unsympathetic to the practical. His course in science and agriculture was regarded as a subterfuge. It was felt advantage had been taken of the Sutton Act [1884] to change the farmers' college into an old-line classical institution." In support of Smith, Ross also wrote that "such criticisms were not wholly just and fair, as some of his students came later to recognize; the young professor was seriously handicapped by inadequate equipment and the inordinate number and variety of subjects he had to teach." Smith obviously met with approval from the trustees, who continued to employ him after he completed his two-year contract.

During Smith's second year at the college, Dr. Welch died. Welch was wintering in California at the time. His body was returned to Iowa and on March 21, 1889, a memorial service was held in the college chapel. Friends and dignitaries honored him as a trusted colleague and a humanitarian. The Ames Woman's Suffrage Association sent a large wreath of white roses that spelled out "Our Friend." Welch was buried in the college cemetery located on the west edge of the campus in a beautiful grove of walnut trees.

The sad opening of the school year of 1889 was just the beginning of turmoil for the faculty. President Chamberlain's unpopular tactics in handling student problems and the strong opposition by the farmers of the state to his programs was enough to force his resignation within a year of Welch's death. In November 1890, Chamberlain retired as president. His resignation was followed by that of several faculty members, including Loren Smith who, as Earle Ross wrote, resigned after learning of opposition to him by some members of the board. Herman Knapp again came to the rescue of the college farm and Professor Stanton took over as acting president.

Smith moved from the Farm House by the end of November 1890 and settled in Washington, D.C., where he died unexpectedly six years later on December 2, 1896. Perhaps by coincidence, when Smith resigned, Professor Barrows asked the trustees to release him from his housing arrangement at the Farm House so he could move his family into Ames. His request was approved in January 1891, and Barrows received a housing allowance of $200 a year in lieu of housing at the Farm House. Barrows continued to work at the college until 1894, when he returned to teaching at Western Reserve in Cleveland, Ohio.

After Smith and the Barrows family moved from the Farm House, the only people known to be living there were two employees of the experiment station: C. G. Gillette, station entomologist, and

G. E. Patrick, station chemist. Both Gillette and Patrick began work at the experiment station in 1888.

The Farm House was home to Seaman Knapp and his family during most of the 1880s. Knapp was one of the most influential members of the college faculty; his efforts on behalf of scientific experiments and demonstration plots resulted in federal legislation for financing experiment stations at land-grant colleges. The Farm House was still a boarding house while Knapp lived there. It became the president's home when Knapp succeeded Dr. Welch as the second president of the college in 1883. Knapp's son, Herman, and daughter-in-law, Mary, lived in the Farm House during its renovation into a duplex in 1886 and later were among the faculty who built their own homes on campus. As the Farm House began its fourth decade of service to the campus, resignations by the college president and numerous faculty members set the scene for an abrupt reversal of the expansion of the college curriculum set in motion by the Sutton Act of 1884. An era of narrow, conservative thinking would shape the college during the 1890s and give the Farm House another of its most distinguished residents.

6 · *The Wilson and Curtiss Years*

*I*n the late fall of 1890, the powerful Iowa Stock Breeders Association delivered several ultimatums to the trustees of the agricultural college. These demands, they believed, would save their "farmers' college" from the liberalized curriculum which evolved under President Chamberlain's direction. These ultimatums eventually resulted in a complete revision of the agriculture program at the school and created a new position by merging the agricultural teaching responsibilities and the running of the experiment station. The candidate backed by the Stock Breeders Association for this new position was James "Tama Jim" Wilson, who would make the Farm House his home during his tenure at the college. His career at the college would extend into the 20th century and his influence would play a significant role in the life of his protégé and successor, Charles F. Curtiss.

James "Tama Jim" Wilson's arrival on the college campus was well planned and orchestrated with the help of Henry "Uncle Henry" Wallace and C. L. Gabrilson. In the fall of 1890 when Chamberlain and Smith resigned from their positions, Wilson, Wallace, and Gabrilson prepared a resolution, which they presented to the Iowa Stock Breeders Association, advocating a complete revision of the course of study in the agriculture program. Their resolution demanded the following: (1) that all courses not directly related to agriculture be eliminated; (2) that the trustees establish a short course in agriculture during the winter months; (3) that they establish a dairy school; and (4) that the experiment station be made a department of the college and maintained as a "distinct department of the college directly for the benefit of farmers, incidentally of students." Because there was no statewide system of high school programs in Iowa, they also demanded that the admission standards be dropped and that a two-year agriculture program be instituted. The association enthusiastically endorsed the resolution and sent it on to the trustees. The trustees made every effort to defend their existing programs but, in their January 1891 meetings, admitted defeat and accepted all the reorganization proposals except the one making the experiment station a department of the college. They did, however, decide to hire one person to teach agriculture and run the experiment station.

To carry out the new program instituted by the trustees, the Stock Breeders Association along with the Dairymen's Association and the State Alliance of Iowa Farmers petitioned the trustees to elect James "Tama Jim" Wilson as professor of agriculture and director of the experiment station. Historian Earle Ross wrote that Henry Wallace, the editor of the *Iowa Homestead* newspaper, and Wilson's lifelong friend, was first approached for this honor but because of prior commitments he deferred to Wilson. It was not the first time Wallace was involved in the selection of the faculty at the college—he was a behind-the-scenes player in the selection of his old family friend, Seaman Knapp, as professor of agriculture back in 1880.

The trustees held their tension-filled January 1891 meetings in packed, smoke-filled rooms. The reorganization of the agriculture program took up the major portion of the meetings followed by the selection of candidates for the new director's position and the presidency. The trustees chose two men the Stock Breeders and Dairymen's Association also supported—Reverend William M. Beardshear of West Des Moines as president and James "Tama Jim" Wilson of Traer as professor of agriculture and director of the experiment station. Wilson received a salary of $2,000 a year and use of the west side of the Farm House vacated by Professor Barrows and his family. The trustees also hired Charles F. Curtiss as station assistant and assigned him the two rooms on the west side of the first floor of the station building as living quarters. They left the question of a tenant for the east side of the Farm House up to Professor Wilson and the Board of Audit.

James Wilson was 56 years old when he accepted the position of professor of agriculture and director of the experiment station. Although Wilson was not a native Iowan, he adopted the nickname "Tama Jim" while living in Tama County, Iowa, to differentiate himself from another James Wilson, a legislator who also hailed from Iowa. He was born in Girwan Parish, Ayrshire, Scotland, in 1835, and

James "Tama Jim" Wilson.
Courtesy of Iowa State University Library/University Archives

Esther Wilbur Wilson (Mrs. James Wilson), ca. 1860s.
Courtesy of Iowa State University Library/University Archives

Flora Wilson.
Published in the New York Times, *April 30, 1899*

was the oldest of 14 children of John and Jean Wilson. The family left Scotland and arrived in America when James was 16. He attended college for one year at Grinnell, Iowa, and later taught school. He claimed to be mostly self-educated and was quoted as saying he learned Roberts's *Rules of Order* from the tailgate of a wagon while husking corn. He was 28 when he married Esther Wilbur in 1863. Wilson served three terms in the Iowa legislature and in 1872 was elected to the first of his three terms in the U.S. House of Representatives. While a member of the House he made friends with a future U.S. president, William McKinley, who would later appoint Wilson his secretary of agriculture. Wilson also developed a lifelong friendship with Henry "Uncle Henry" Wallace. Both were early critics of the agricultural program at the Iowa Agricultural College.

Wilson's appointment at the college was finalized in January 1891, which left him little time to get his family moved from their home in Traer and into the Farm House before classes began on March 1. The Wilsons were advised to bring their own furniture to the college because most of the bedding that was in the Farm House (except for one feather bed) had been sold in 1888. Four of the five Wilson boys came with the family to the college and only the eldest son, Ward, remained in Traer to manage the family farm. Ward was a class-

Charles F. Curtiss, ca.
1890s.
Reminiscenses of Iowa Agricultural College, *1897*

mate of Charles Curtiss, and was pleased to hear of Curtiss's appointment as his father's assistant at the experiment station. Mrs. Wilson would miss her eldest son because it was Ward who especially supported and encouraged his mother during the long years that Mr. Wilson was away in Washington. The Wilsons' only daughter, Flora, was attending school at Coe College and planned to transfer to the Iowa Agricultural College in September. The Wilsons also invited several nephews to live with them so they could attend classes at the college.

Mrs. Wilson presided over a busy, lively household. She required help running the house and hired several students to work in the kitchen. Mrs. Wilson had not been in the best of health when she arrived at the college and the poor condition of the Farm House added stress to the family's home life. In May Professor Wilson went to the trustees to ask for money to repair the house. Nothing had been done to the Farm House since 1886 when it was converted into a duplex. While other houses on campus were heated with furnaces, the Farm House still was heated with a few room stoves, leaving most of the house uncomfortably cold. The privy behind the house was now 25 years old and the bricks on the outside of the house were beginning to show the effects of the harsh winters. While the trustees were in complete sympathy with Wilson, they were unwilling to put more money into the Farm House. As a compromise, the trustees increased Wilson's salary another $500 a year with the understanding that he would make the repairs to the Farm House at his own expense, which he did. There is no record, however, of what these improvements were.

The Wilsons moved to the college campus the same year that the train connecting the campus with the city of Ames made its appearance. The train tracks for the "Dinkey," as it was called by everyone, ran directly behind the Farm House and across campus to the Main Building and the Hub Station. The sound of the train and the rattling across the tracks could be felt in the Farm House, but it was a welcome addition to the campus. The train made it possible to travel in comfort from the Ames depot to the college within 15 minutes, and it brought the college and townspeople closer together.

Wilson's daughter, Flora, arrived at the college for the 1891 fall session. The Wilson family celebrated Peter Wilson's graduation from

Motor approach to the campus from the east.
Courtesy of Iowa State University Library/University Archives

The east side of the Farm House, 1905. Skylights are visible on the
roof. Dinkey railroad tracks are in the lower right.
Courtesy of Iowa State University Library/University Archives

the college in November 1891 and looked forward to Flora's graduation the following year. Flora entered the college at a time when debating societies were the rage. Students could now spend their free time in a variety of activities. They could attend on-campus dances (which were previously banned) and participate in lawn socials, croquet, baseball, fishing parties, or buggy rides to Boone for a secret rendezvous. Student life was still regimented but no longer under the constant, watchful eye of the college president. By 1891 the main central campus had manicured lawns and paved walkways. Money from the legislature and the federal government created a building boom during the 1880s and the college now had a veterinary hospital, gymnasium, student hospital, creamery, 10 faculty houses, several student boarding houses, an English office building, mechanical and chemical laboratories, and Morrill Hall, which was dedicated shortly after Wilson arrived on campus. The Main Building, once deemed unlivable by the students, and the new Morrill Hall had indoor plumbing, central heating, telephones, and electricity generated by the college plant. These utilities would gradually be extended to other buildings on campus, including the faculty houses and the Farm House.

In January of 1892, the trustees gave the Wilsons the use of the entire Farm House for their family. It is not known whether anyone was renting rooms on the east side of the house. Wilson's nephews lived at the Farm House while they were attending school and may have rented these rooms from him, but it is more likely Wilson provided them with housing at his own expense. When the trustees gave Wilson the use of the entire Farm House, he again asked for additional funds to remodel the house, this time back into a single-family unit. The trustees, however, made it clear that any further improvements to the Farm House would have to be made at Wilson's expense. It is likely the Wilson family began using the newer east kitchen at this time and converted the west kitchen to another use. This required considerable remodeling, which might have included enclosing the original east kitchen exterior doorway and connecting it to the back entry room. Although it is commonly believed that the two west rooms in the main section of the house were converted to a large parlor by the Curtiss family, it could have been done while the Wilsons lived in the house to create a large room for entertaining. James Wilson was extremely proud of Flora's musical accomplishments and a large parlor would have been ideal for the musical events she planned and hosted at the house.

During Wilson's second year at the college, a great tragedy struck the family. The August 4, 1892, edition of the *Ames Intelligencer* reported on Mrs. Wilson's untimely death:

> Yesterday afternoon the residents of Ames and vicinity were startled by the news that Mrs. Wilson, wife of Prof. Wilson, had been drowned in the creek on the college farm. Mrs. Wilson was last seen a short time before noon when after a visit to the office she returned home and gave directions concerning the family dinner....Her health being delicate and tho some consider the drowning accidental the general theory is suicide due to insanity. Mrs. Wilson has become greatly beloved during her residence here and universal sympathy is felt for the family in their sad loss.

Services for Esther Wilson were conducted in the parlor at the Farm House, after which the family traveled to Traer, Iowa, where Esther was buried near other family members.

It was Flora who comforted her father during the months following her mother's death and helped keep the family together. Her own graduation from college in November 1892 was quietly celebrated at home with family. After graduation, Flora continued to live at home with her father and brothers at the Farm House and later accepted a position at the college library. The college yearbook of 1896 described Flora's many talents:

> She is decidedly domestic, and has been her father's housekeeper ever since the death of her mother— like a true and noble daughter and sister, keeping one of the most perfect homes and filling dutifully and lovingly the place of her mother. She has always had a taste and natural ability for journalism, and has written for publication several pleasing stories....She is also a vocalist of marked ability. In brief she is a young person whom all like on account of her winning ways and natural talents.

A newspaper article printed after Wilson accepted a position in Washington in 1897 described Flora as "a slender girl, with dark hair and blue eyes, and the white skin which usually goes with that combination." The article also noted her musical abilities and her "rarely sweet high soprano [voice which]. . . has had careful culture." It was to James Wilson's credit that he did not neglect his daughter's musical career while she was keeping house for him at the college. He saw that she had every opportunity to travel during winter vacations to train with professional voice instructors in the East. Flora in turn used her musical abilities to entertain her friends at the college. According to one newspaper article, "Wilson's home has always been the musical center of the college, and Miss Wilson's musicales have often brought together some of the finest musicians of the State."

While Flora maintained the Farm House as home for the Wilson family, James Wilson put his energies into strengthening the agricultural program at the college. Wilson later wrote that he was distressed when he arrived on campus and found that only one student, a Mr. J. H. Sheppherd, was enrolled in the agriculture program. "Uncle Henry" Wallace recalled that "when Wilson took charge agriculture students were 'hayseeds.'...In the six years he was at Ames he...laid the foundation upon which has been built probably the greatest all-around agricultural college in the country." Louis Pammel, a pioneer botanist at Iowa State Agricultural College, remembered Wilson as a "great man in the classroom and as a public speaker,...[a] precise and intensively interesting man who believes in Agriculture as an enlightened occupation."

Wilson is described in the college yearbook of 1893 as a man who put his "whole-souled nature into the work for the advancement of Iowa farmers, old and young. His unselfish public spirit manifests itself on every worthy occasion where money or speeches are in order." Wilson took a great interest in the students and later wrote that he had shown a particular interest in one student, George Washington Carver, the first African-American to graduate from the college. He did so in 1894 with a degree in agriculture. Carver was a frequent visitor to the Wilson's Traer farm and was a familiar face at the Farm House. After Carver graduated, Wilson encouraged Charles Curtiss to hire him as his assistant at the experiment station, where Carver worked until he accepted a position at Tuskegee Institute in Alabama.

In 1894 Carver graduated from the college and began his position at the experiment station, Dr. Barrows resigned from the college and returned to Ohio, Flora Wilson began her position as librarian at the college, and the trustees abolished the position of assistant professor of agriculture and authorized Professor Wilson to hire a competent farm foreman for $50 a month. The college farm survived the drought of 1894 and the college sued the railroad over the number of cattle killed on the railroad tracks by trains, which the trustees said were a nuisance on the campus. In 1895 Charles Curtiss received a promotion to full professor of animal husbandry and assistant director of the experiment station and a salary increase to $1,800 a year. Lights were extended to the creamery and Agriculture Hall in 1895 and the trustees authorized a small platform and station stop for the "Dinkey" motorline behind the Farm House.

During the six years the Wilsons lived at the Farm House, James Wilson made several major improvements to the house. In 1896 he installed a furnace in the cellar, which finally connected each and every room in the Farm House to a blast of heat even during the coldest months. To install pipes to the radiators in the east kitchen and back entry, a portion of the foundation was removed from the northeast wall of the cellar to provide access to the crawl space under these rooms. Later, when time obscured the true reason for the break in the wall, this dirt floor under the east kitchen became the scene for stories of a hiding place for runaway slaves during the Civil War. Wilson also installed water closets in the house in 1896 and had the brick privy, which had been in use since the 1860s, torn down. Three water closets or bathrooms are known to have existed in the house in the 1890s, but the only known location was at the end of the second floor hallway, between the southeast and southwest front bedrooms. That bathroom has since been removed and the area is now a part of the hall. Wilson later requested reimbursement for these expenses when he left the college for Washington.

In 1896, Wilson's old friend and former colleague in Congress, William McKinley, became the 25th president of the United States. According to the *Ames Evening Times,* McKinley sent a registered letter to Wilson on January 28, 1897, asking Wilson to meet him in Canton, Ohio. Wilson immediately left the college and traveled by train to Ohio, where McKinley asked him to be his secretary of agriculture. Wilson spent some agonizing days considering his obligations to the college before accepting McKinley's offer. He offered his resignation to the trustees on February 4, 1897. Herman Knapp later wrote that "'Tama Jim' called us together in the south-west second floor of the Agriculture Building to announce he had accepted the position in McKinley's cabinet."

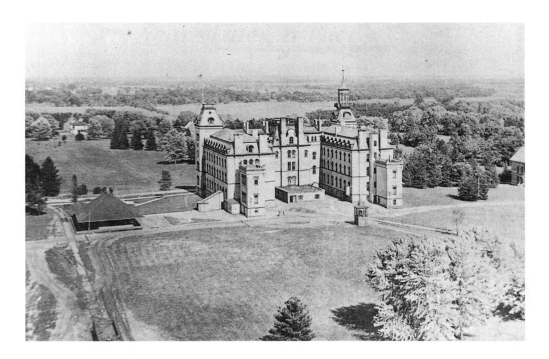

[ABOVE LEFT] View of west campus from Old Main, ca. 1890s. *Center, left to right:* East Cottage, West Cottage, Chemistry Hall, Engineering Building, and workshop.
Courtesy of Iowa State University Library/University Archives

[ABOVE] Old Main, looking east, 1897.
Courtesy of Iowa State University Library/University Archives

[LEFT] Military drill on central campus, ca. 1900.
Courtesy of Iowa State University Library/University Archives

Two weeks later the Ames community gave Wilson one of the most extravagant and memorable dinner receptions the town had ever seen. It was reported to be a nonpartisan affair and the reception took place at the Odd Fellows and Masonic Hall in downtown Ames followed by a sit-down dinner for 235 at the Steven-Budd Building. A committee of volunteers hastily arranged the event and decorated the reception hall. A green banner with huge letters made of corn spelling out "Tama Jim" hung across the stage. The *Ames Evening Times* reported it was a "veritable love feast, a hearty hand-shaking time." The reception and dinner brought together friends of Wilson's from Ames and the college, state and local dignitaries, and visiting members of the U.S. Congress. Wilson's reply to the congratulatory speeches was sincere and humble. He said in part,

> I am to some extent unmanned tonight. More kind things have been said of me than I ever expected in my life. When I was a boy and was following the plow, and the team went right ahead of its own accords, I used to build castles in the air, but you have built an edifice tonight much higher than any I ever dared to build. A seat in the cabinet is not the highest honor in the world—not as high as I have received tonight. You have made me utterly bankrupt in gratitude.

Wilson had little more than a week after the reception to put his office in order at the college and arrange for his trip to Washington. He recommended that Charles Curtiss be promoted to take his place as director of the experiment station and professor of agriculture. Wilson also asked to be reimbursed for the furnace he installed in the Farm House and for his expenses in having the privy torn down and the bricks removed. Instead of accepting Wilson's resignation the trustees asked Wilson to take an unpaid leave from the college and appointed Curtiss to take over Wilson's duties beginning March 1, 1897.

Wilson left the college and headed for Washington the first week in March 1897. Flora remained at the Farm House until the end of the spring session when she resigned from her position at the library. The previous year Flora's brother James W. graduated from the college and her brother Jasper was then completing his final year at the college. It was up to Flora and her brothers to pack the family possessions and move everything they would not be taking to Washington back to their family home in Traer.

Wilson kept in touch with his family via weekly letters encouraging Flora to hasten her arrival in Washington. Wilson's first cabinet meeting with President McKinley was March 9, 1897. Wilson made an impressive entrance dressed all in black, with a silk top hat and black cape overcoat. He was six feet, three inches tall with deep-set eyes and heavy gray eyebrows and beard. When he spoke it was with a Scots dialect combined with a New England twang. Wilson's work in Washington did not prevent him from keeping in touch with the college. Over the years he wrote copious letters to Charles Curtiss and sent him words of encouragement when Curtiss began to question his continued employment at the college. Wilson continued on indefinite leave and became dean of agriculture in November 1897, a position he held until 1902 when Curtiss again took over for him.

James W. Wilson, ca. 1895. *Iowa Agricultural College* BOMB, *1896*

The trustees appointed Charles Curtiss professor of agriculture and acting director of the experiment station on February 4, 1897, the same day Wilson resigned. Curtiss received an adjusted salary of $2,000 a year and the Farm House as his residence. While Charles Curtiss was extremely pleased with his promotion, his wife Olive was not at all happy about the prospects of moving from their new home in Ames to the campus. Curtiss informed the trustees of their plans to continue living in Ames. This notification apparently upset the trustees who made it clear to Curtiss that, if he wanted to accept the new position, which included responsibility for the college farm and livestock, he would have to live on the campus in the Farm House. The trustees gave Curtiss an ultimatum: either live at the Farm House or no promotion. Curtiss agreed to the trustees' demands. In an effort to smooth the transition for the Curtiss family, the trustees authorized extensive repairs to the house and declared it an "emergency matter." They also recommended tearing down the attached woodshed, which they said was in danger of falling and was a haven for rats.

The Curtiss home in Ames was a marked contrast

Jasper Wilson, ca. 1890s. Reminiscenses of Iowa Agricultural Collegc, *1897*

to the Farm House. Since the arrival of the "Dinkey" motorline in 1891, which provided regular daily service between Ames and the college, many of the faculty members chose to build their homes in Ames. Members of the faculty who lived in town enjoyed a lively social life which was often separate from the college. Curtiss was one of those who chose to live in town. He built his home at 712 Duff Avenue in 1892 in anticipation of his marriage to Olive Wilson in 1893. (The house is still lived in today and is being restored by its owners.) It was a large Victorian house with a wide sweeping front porch, a neatly landscaped yard, indoor plumbing, and central heat. Wide sidewalks connected the house to the other homes in the growing neighborhood.

The Farm House on the other hand was 30 years old, isolated on the farm side of the college campus with a dusty road going by the side of the house and a railroad track running through the backyard. Olive probably worried about the safety of her two small girls as much as she fretted about giving up her beautiful new home in town. There is some question as to when the Curtiss family actually moved into the Farm House. Wilson wrote to Curtiss in the summer of 1897 inquiring if he had moved his family to the Farm House yet, but there is no record of Curtiss's response. Although they retained

The Curtiss home at 712 Duff Ave., Ames, Iowa, ca. 1895.
Ames Intelligencer, *Souvenir Edition, 1897. Courtesy of Ames Public Library*

Charles F. Curtiss in a buggy in front of the Farm House, ca. 1900.
Courtesy of Iowa State University Library/University Archives

ownership of their home at 712 Duff Avenue until 1903, it is generally believed that the family was settled in the Farm House by 1897. It is unlikely the house remained empty after Flora Wilson moved to Traer in the summer of 1897 even though it was undergoing extensive remodeling. It is possible Charles Curtiss stayed at the Farm House while it was being repaired and his wife and two young daughters joined him later in the year.

The Curtiss children, three-year-old Ruth and baby Edith, only one year old at the time of their move to the Farm House, were both born in Ames and enjoyed the company of the large extended Curtiss family, most of whom lived in the nearby town of Nevada where their father had lived as a child. Charles Curtiss was not a native Iowan but came to Iowa from Nora, Illinois, with his parents shortly after his birth on December 10, 1863. He grew up on the family farm in Story County, Iowa, and graduated from Nevada High School. While attending Iowa State Agricultural College he met his future wife—a classmate—Olive (Ollie) Wilson of Harper, Keokuk County, Iowa.

The Curtiss family at the family home in Nevada, Iowa, ca. 1905.
Charles Curtiss is on the extreme left in the back row and Olive Curtiss
is to the right of him. Helen and Edith are fifth and sixth from the left
in the front row; Ruth is at the extreme right.
Courtesy of Jeanette Rex

They made a striking couple. He was tall—six feet, three inches—and
seemed to tower over diminutive Olive, who was nine inches shorter.
They both graduated with the class of 1887, but Charles came to the
unfavorable attention of the trustees during a review of his course-
work because he was behind in both trigonometry and surveying,
which he presumably completed in time to graduate. After graduation
Charles accepted a position with the state of Iowa, worked on the
family farm and, two years before his marriage to Olive, began working at the college with "Tama Jim" Wilson.

Curtiss took over as acting director of the experiment station in
March 1897, saying he felt confident in accepting the position as he
would have three good assistants, one of whom was James W. Wilson,
a son of "Tama Jim" Wilson. Curtiss developed a strong reputation
with the Iowa farmers early in his career, although some doubted his
recommendation to plant soybeans in Iowa after the 1894 drought
wiped out the corn crop. (Soybeans are now one of Iowa's top
money-making crops.)

In November 1897, the trustees changed "Tama Jim" Wilson's title to dean of the agriculture faculty and promoted Charles Curtiss
from acting director to director of the experiment station. Wilson and
Curtiss kept in close contact with weekly letters about college business, but it was Curtiss who carried out the programs and did the
work.

Curtiss is credited with organizing the Department of Agricultural Journalism and establishing the first agricultural extension departments. He was one of the organizers of the International Livestock Exposition in 1900 and he became an expert in the livestock
judging arena. His judging cane became his constant companion; Curtiss rarely went for a walk across campus without it. He was also an
expert horseman and was happiest when making the rounds of the
college farm astride his favorite horse.

Charles Curtiss in front of the Farm House, ca. 1905.
Courtesy of Iowa State University Library/University Archives

While the farm was still an important part of the college, its role in the everyday life of the students had diminished since the late 1880s. Agricultural experiments were still an important part of the college curriculum but were carried on year-round in modern greenhouses. It was no longer necessary for the college to follow the natural planting and harvesting schedules. Classroom buildings were now thoroughly heated so classes could be held in relative comfort during the cold Iowa winters. In 1898 the name of the college changed to reflect its growth. Iowa State Agricultural College and Model Farm became known as Iowa State College of Agriculture and Mechanic Arts. Beginning in 1900, the school year started in September and ended in June, replacing the 30-year tradition of beginning the school year in March and closing in November.

The 30 years of growth in the college also meant 30 years of hard wear on the older buildings on campus. Several of the original faculty homes were moved, some more than once, to make room for new buildings. Often smaller buildings were combined to create new facilities. Fortunately, the Farm House was spared major reconstruction but its continued repair was dependent on the goodwill of the trustees and the finances of the college. The repairs to the interior of the house in 1897 were mostly cosmetic. They included wallpapering the first-floor rooms (a later letter dated 1902 from Curtiss to President Stanton notes that the wallpapering was done by Hartsung of Des Moines), repainting the woodwork, and repairing the floors, which included a fresh coat of brown paint. (During a 1992 repair to the flooring in the central hallway on the second floor the original floorboards were exposed and found to be painted with a brown paint.) The remaining woodshed attached to the north side of the house was removed and the north doorway in the old west kitchen was bricked over with bricks found in the cellar that were left over from the original construction of the house. The exterior soft redbrick walls of the house received a coat of white paint to help prevent further deterioration. The following year electricity was extended to the house and a new, smaller front porch replaced the elegant but dilapidated Italianate porch which had spanned the front of the house since 1865.

While the Curtiss family enjoyed the use of the Farm House for their home, there was also a constant stream of visitors and renters sharing the house with them. Olive's sister, Elmina Wilson, who taught at the college, lived with the Curtiss family in 1900. She was a great help to Olive with the young girls and was there when a third daughter, Helen, was born at the Farm House on September 14, 1901.

The Curtiss family also boarded John Alexander Craig, professor of animal husbandry; Helen Knapp, daughter of Seaman and Maria Knapp, who was now an assistant librarian; and Vina Elethe Clark, librarian. As the girls grew up and required more space, fewer boarders stayed with the family.

In 1902, James "Tama Jim" Wilson resigned from his position as dean of agriculture but retained ties to the college, still preferring to be on official leave. President Beardshear, with the trustees' approval, appointed Charles Curtiss as Wilson's replacement to be the second dean of agriculture. In August 1902, Main Building was severely damaged by fire and, most shockingly, President Beardshear died unexpectedly on August 5. He and Charles Curtiss were good friends, as were their wives and children, and Beardshear's death was a loss that left the campus in mourning and set in motion the prospect of a college presidency for Charles Curtiss.

Edgar Stanton became acting president at Beardshear's death and was considered his likely successor although there was also a serious move to elect Curtiss as president of the college. On April 29, 1903, James "Tama Jim" Wilson wrote to Curtiss,

> I have just had a letter from Mr. Hungerford [trustee] asking me to speak out with regard to the College situation. He is, I think, considering you seriously for President. I have given him every reason I can think of why you should be the man, and now I want to say to you that if it comes, you accept it. You are the best man for it. It will be you or someone from outside the campus, and I fear a calamity if the Board goes outside.

Wilson also wrote to Reverend R. H. Dolliver on May 9, 1903, saying that Curtiss was the unanimous choice of the farmers of Iowa. To Trustee W. K. Boardman, Wilson wrote on June 10, 1903, "The best thing they [trustees] can do is to put in Curtiss, but he hesitates to come out as a candidate, and what will happen I do not know."

Neither Stanton nor Curtiss were the trustees' final choice. Instead they chose a compromise candidate, Albert B. Storms, who became the sixth president of the college in the summer of 1903. Wilson wrote to Curtiss on July 27, 1903,

I want to say to you that the late developments at
Ames have taken a good deal of the heart out of me,
as far as your work there is concerned....Your election would have done more to encourage work along
these lines in college and station than any one thing,
but the conclusion they have come to is, that no man
educated along these lines is fit for a college president....There is a good deal at the college Storms can
do. If he does not become positively hostile to you,
there is a good deal that you can do.

Whatever Curtiss thought about President Storms, his decision
to remain at the college was greatly influenced by Wilson's encouragement of his work.

Curtiss put his energy into the development of student livestock
judging teams, which he had encouraged since he hired Willard
Kennedy away from the University of Illinois in 1900. It was Curtiss
who gained a place for college livestock judging teams in the international competitions and his office in Agriculture Hall was soon
lined with trophies won by Iowa State College teams. Curtiss also
maintained another office in his home at the Farm House. There the
room was lined with leaded glass-front bookcases on which rested a
bust of Dante and a photograph of a smiling President Beardshear.
His home library was his sanctuary away from his formal office and
was a room remembered by a niece for Curtiss's collection of small
iron animals which he would remove from the shelves for her to
hold.

Curtiss's Farm House library was one of the rooms Curtiss wrote
about to acting president Stanton in March 1902, asking for funds to
rewallpaper, as the wallpaper put up in 1897 was peeling off the
walls in large sections. He estimated the cost of the library wallpaper
at 25 cents a roll but asked for more expensive wallpaper for the dining room for which he offered to help pay. Curtiss also asked for
funds to install a fireplace in his library which was to be connected
to an existing chimney in the northeast corner of the room. (The fireplace was removed during renovations in 1948 because of safety concerns.) All these repairs he estimated would cost $125 and he asked
that they be completed by the fall of 1902. A photograph of his library was later featured in a 1907 issue of the *Iowa Agriculturalist*
magazine as an example of tasteful decoration. Visitors to the house
recalled that there was always a fire in the fireplace and one student
who rented a room with the Curtiss family remembered that it was

The Curtiss library in the Farm House, ca. 1906.
Iowa Agriculturalist, *1907. Courtesy of Iowa State University Library/University
Archives*

his job to get the fire going each morning before Curtiss came downstairs.

While the library was Charles Curtiss's domain, Olive's touch
was evident throughout the rest of the house. Lace curtains lined the
first-floor windows and oriental carpets covered the bedroom floors.
Olive enjoyed entertaining her many friends for luncheons, and her
dining room was noted for its elegant service of Haviland china and
beautiful cut glass displayed in the china cabinet. Mrs. Curtiss was
one of the organizers of the informal afternoon teas at the homes of
the faculty wives that led to the establishment of the Priscilla Club,
later known as the Faculty Women's Club at the college, which still
flourishes today. She was also a charter member of the A.A. chapter
of the P.E.O., as were many of her friends in the Priscilla Club.

[ABOVE] Reunion of P.E.O. group, October 20, 1942. *Back row, left to right:* Mrs. Harriman, Mrs. George Hultz (Gladys Meade's Mother), and Stella Hunter. *Front row:* Mrs. Noble, Mrs. Sarah Fitchpatrick McElyea, Mrs. Olive Curtiss, Mrs. Alma Hamilton (*holding cane*), and Mrs. Alice Marston. *Courtesy of A.A. Chapter, P.E.O., Ames, Iowa*

[ABOVE RIGHT] The Curtiss children on the porch of the Farm House, ca. 1905. *Iowa Agricultural College* BOMB, *1905*

[RIGHT] Farm House, ca. 1908, with a tree house in the west yard. *Courtesy of Iowa State University Library/University Archives*

In 1909, seven years after Curtiss was considered for the presidency of the college, the Iowa legislature dissolved the Board of Trustees who had governed the Iowa State College since 1859 and combined the governing authorities of all three state colleges under one Board of Education. The following year President Storms resigned, saying that the Board of Education would be better off with a president they selected. This time, Curtiss was not among the candidates for president, and Raymond M. Pearson became the seventh president of the college.

Before Storms left the college, Curtiss wrote to him requesting funds for major repairs at the Farm House. (Curtiss was really the one who saved the Farm House from destruction long before it was considered for a similar fate in the 1970s.) His letter to President Storms in June 1909 suggests that the house was seriously being considered for demolition at that time. He wrote,

> A coat of plaster finish would greatly improve the appearance of the building and put it in a much more permanent condition. The house has been connected with the central heating plant, and the water system put in good condition. It is not likely now that it will be necessary to remove the house, and I believe that it is valuable enough to make it worth while to put it in good condition, with a view to permanent serviceability in the future.

Curtiss also requested a screened porch for the west side of the house, as designed by Proudfoot and Bird of Des Moines, but added, "The porch is not an immediate necessity....I think the other part of the work, however, is very urgent....Some of the floors should be repaired and have hardwood borders, and the saving on the painting will be needed on the floors."

This request for floor repairs resulted in the beautiful oak flooring which was placed over the original wide-plank floorboards throughout most of the house. Although a parlor fireplace is not mentioned in his request, it is generally believed the fireplace and the French doors on either side of the fireplace were part of this remodeling project. Photographs taken around 1912, when the stucco project was completed, show the new screened porch. This porch became a favorite place for afternoon teas given by Olive. There, she and her visitors had a sweeping view across the campus and could keep a watchful eye on their children.

The children of the campus families had their own special

The Farm House with west porch addition, ca. 1912, after stucco had
been applied to the bricks.
Courtesy of Iowa State University Library/University Archives

Farm House, ca. 1912.
Courtesy of Iowa State University Library/University Archives

Helen Curtiss and pigs, ca.
1912.
*Courtesy of Iowa State University Library/University
Archives*

places to meet, and one of their favorite spots was the tree house that Charles Curtiss built for his daughters, Helen, Edith, and Ruth, in the huge tree on the west side yard of the Farm House. The three Curtiss girls grew up on campus with children from the Beyer, Marston, Sloss, and Mortensen families, all of whom now attended school with the Ames children. One of Helen Curtiss's friends was Marie Mortensen, who moved to the college campus with her family in 1907 when she was six years old, the same age as Helen. Marie and Helen were always looking for something adventurous to do. Marie later recalled the wonderful afternoons she and Helen spent as children riding up and down the elevator in Agriculture Hall (now Curtiss Hall) to the great annoyance of the faculty and their parents. Marie also remembered with delight the closet full of games and chalk in the Farm House parlor and how she and Helen waited until the dean had left for his office before venturing into the parlor to spread the paper dolls on the oriental carpet for an afternoon of fun. In later years the parlor was the center of family parties and a beautiful red mahogany baby grand piano graced the northwest corner of the room.

While Dean Curtiss was a very formal man and could appear quite aloof, he took great pleasure in his children. One afternoon the dean arrived home while the children were playing with the water hose and young Helen accidentally sprayed her father, getting his clothing completely soaked. Without comment the dean went inside, changed his clothing, reappeared outside, picked up the hose, squirted Helen, and walked off to his office without saying a word to the astonished children.

In 1904 Curtiss purchased a 330-acre farm southwest of the college where he raised shorthorn cattle, Berkshire pigs, and Percheron horses. Helen, who shared her father's love of animals, was a frequent visitor to the farm, which Curtiss named Rookwood. (Curtiss eventually gave the farm to the college and the land now is the site of the ISU Curtiss Farm and also is used for experimental plots by the university faculty.) While all three Curtiss girls enjoyed the farm, it was Helen who loved horses and became an excellent rider. Even as a child Helen was a familiar sight on campus, leading parades astride her small pony. In the winter, when it was too cold to ride horseback,

Dean Curtiss often arranged for a hay wagon to take the children around the college farm for a brisk ride after which they returned to the Farm House for a bowl of Mrs. Curtiss's hot oyster stew. Oyster stew was then all the rage and Mrs. Curtiss's was considered among the best.

Josephine Hungerford Dodds, a frequent visitor to the Farm House, later wrote that "Mrs. Curtiss was a fine hostess, capable in every way, friendly to the myriad of people who crossed her threshold....she was a gourmet cook. Nothing was too much trouble. In that old kitchen she achieved miracles."

Mrs. Curtiss also worked miracles on the rest of the house. Mrs. Dodds continued that the house "had an air of great luxury, with polished floors, oriental rugs, and long gold draperies at the French doors...Books lined the library walls,...the furniture was dark oak,...the dining room contained a large table, sideboard loaded with silver, china closets with glass doors."

Edith and Helen on a pony, ca. 1906.
Farm House Museum Archives. Courtesy of David L. Shugart

[RIGHT] Helen, Edith, and
Ruth Curtiss in front of
Botany Hall.
Published in the Iowa Agricul-
turalist, *October 1908*

[BOTTOM LEFT] Edith Curtiss
Shugart, ca. 1940s.
Courtesy of David L. Shugart

[BOTTOM RIGHT] Edith Cur-
tiss, ca. 1916.
*Courtesy of Iowa State Univer-
sity Library/University
Archives*

[ABOVE LEFT] Helen Curtiss, ca. 1915.
Courtesy of Iowa State University Library/University Archives

[ABOVE RIGHT] Helen Curtiss Whittaker, ca. 1976, standing in the southeast bedroom on the second floor of the Farm House, where she said she had been born.
Courtesy of Neva Petersen

[LEFT] Ruth Curtiss (*left*) and Mary Knapp, ca. 1917.
Courtesy of Iowa State University Library/University Archives

Gates on the back walk at the Farm House that were designed by
Helen Curtiss, ca. 1925.
Farm House Museum Archives. Courtesy of David L. Shugart

Panoramic view of cam-
pus, looking north, 1913.
Courtesy of Iowa State Univer-
sity Library/University
Archives

This was the Farm House James "Tama Jim" Wilson saw when he visited the college in 1913 following his retirement from his Cabinet position in Washington, D.C. Charles Curtiss and President Pearson invited Wilson to Ames for "one last celebration on his retirement" and invited him to stay at the Farm House. Wilson wrote to both of them saying he would be there after March 4 for a week or ten days as "I am here on leave of absence from Ames, and I suppose it would be entirely right on returning to Iowa that I go back to Ames and report." Wilson's daughter Flora, who had been his companion and hostess for the past 16 years, chose to remain in Washington and did not return to Iowa with her father. Wilson did stay with the Curtiss family at the Farm House during his 1913 visit before retiring to his farm in Traer, where he died on August 26, 1920.

The year before his death, Wilson sent his very best wishes to Charles and Olive on the marriage of their daughter Edith to classmate Jack Shugart on April 26, 1919. The wedding took place at the Farm House, which was decorated with pink and lavender flowers, palms, and ferns. It was a lovely, simple ceremony; family and friends gathered around the center of the library while Edith and Jack exchanged their wedding vows. Four years later, in 1923, Helen, the youngest and the last of the Curtiss daughters to graduate from Iowa State College, moved from the Farm House. Of the three daughters, Helen was the one who friends remembered as most mischievous and vivacious, constantly surrounded by friends. Her Sunday evening waffle parties at the Farm House were legendary and the garden gates she designed as a senior class project would grace the back walk of the Farm House until the 1940s.

The house was never empty, even after their three daughters moved away; Charles and Olive continued to open their home to nieces and nephews who stayed with them while attending classes at the college. One niece, Phyllis Curtiss, who roomed with the family during the 1920s, met her future husband, Allen W. Perry, at the college and his memory of visits to the house give a warm impression

of Phyllis and the bustling household that always seemed to surround the Curtiss family. To help with entertaining Mrs. Curtiss always employed several young students from the college. An invitation to her luncheons was greatly prized.

It was during the 1930s that Olive and Charles moved down to the first floor of the Farm House. There are conflicting accounts of when they first used the old west kitchen as a bedroom (some suggest Olive moved into this room after the turn of the century because she found the stairs difficult to climb due to her ill health). Charles had a large tub installed in the room located between the east kitchen and their bedroom because he hated showers. They also used this room as a laundry room and it is now the back entry room of the house for the public. Few additional improvements were made to the Farm House during the 1920s except for a garage added in 1926 to the back of the house where once the wooden washroom was attached.

In 1924 Henry C. Wallace, son of "Uncle Henry" Wallace, died while serving as U.S. secretary of agriculture in Calvin Coolidge's Cabinet. Charles Curtiss was one of those mentioned to take his place. Although Curtiss did not receive the appointment, he thought it an honor just to be considered.

Curtiss retired as dean of agriculture in 1932 and relinquished his duties as head of the experiment station the following year. The college honored Curtiss with a lavish testimonial dinner on June 10, 1934, held at the Memorial Union on campus. Over 600 dignitaries and friends attended the evening event. Dr. John H. Sheppherd, who was the only student enrolled in the agriculture program in 1891 when Wilson and Curtiss came to the college, presented a portrait of Dean Curtiss painted by Robert W. Grafton to the college, on behalf of the 1891 graduating class. Dr. Raymond Hughes, president of Iowa State College, accepted the gift and C. L. Burlingham gave the main address, entitled "One Man's Work," which he wrote based on Charles Curtiss's career at the college.

While retired from his administrative duties at the college, Charles Curtiss continued to do research and lecture at the college until 1937. As professor emeritus of agriculture and professor emeritus of the experiment station he continued to maintain an office in the Agriculture Building until his death.

Charles Curtiss always gave the impression of a polished, Victorian gentleman, even in his later years, but his manner could be short and curt. J. C. "Shorty" Schilletter, an employee of the college and friend of Curtiss, remembered one eventful trip he took with his wife, Lennadore, and the Curtiss family to Minnesota. At one point during their trip Charles became impatient with them and drove off in his car, leaving them stranded at the hotel and forcing them to make their way back to Ames on the bus. Charles's abrupt manner didn't dim the friendship between Lennadore and Olive, nor did it particularly irk J. C. Schilletter, who said it was just part of Charles's character.

Even after Curtiss retired from his administrative duties at the college, he and Olive continued to live at the Farm House. Dr. Kildee, who replaced Curtiss as dean of agriculture, did not want to move to the Farm House because he was comfortably settled in his own home on campus. The Farm House was, in fact, then known as the Curtiss House, as it had been for over 30 years. Sometime after Curtiss retired as dean, he began paying $60 a month rent to the college for the use of the Farm House. Some of the upstairs rooms were rented to faculty, most of whom stayed only a short time. However, one faculty member, Dr. Elizabeth Hoyt, began renting at the Curtiss House in 1936 and remained there until 1948.

Olive Curtiss, who had spent 46 years of her married life at the Farm House, died in 1943. After Olive's death, Mary Skarshaug who had been a friend and housekeeper for the Curtiss family, continued to look after the house for Charles. As his health declined and he required the care of a nurse, Polly Gibbs from Ames was hired to attend him during the day. Charles died at the Farm House on July 30, 1947, 50 years after moving into the house with his young family. His funeral services were held in the Episcopal Church on Lincoln Way in Ames where Senator Gillette spoke briefly about Curtiss's accomplishments. Helen and Ruth, the surviving daughters, attended the services with other family members. (Daughter Edith died in 1944.) Charles Curtiss was buried in the college cemetery next to his wife, Olive, amid the century-old oak trees and the graves of former friends and colleagues. After Charles Curtiss's funeral, the family held a household sale, scattering the family's furniture and possessions. Several people who purchased items at this sale have since returned them to the Farm House, where they are on display. It is hoped that other Curtiss family items purchased at this sale will eventually find their way back to the Farm House.

In October 1947, Dr. Kildee sent Helen Curtiss Whittaker a copy of a September 16 resolution that the staff and president of the college had unanimously approved. The resolution honored Dean Curtiss's lifelong work and renamed Agriculture Hall "Curtiss Hall" in his memory. In 1958 the Cowboy Hall of Fame inducted Charles Curtiss into its ranks because, they said, he "brought understanding between farmers and the men of science." It was a tribute Charles Curtiss especially would have enjoyed receiving. James "Tama Jim" Wilson certainly would have concurred with this assessment of Curtiss's work and would have seen it as the ultimate compliment to both of them for their efforts on behalf of the American farmer.

In 1891 James "Tama Jim" Wilson and Charles F. Curtiss began their careers at Iowa State Agricultural College during a time of controversy and conflict between the farmers of the state and the trustees of the college. Wilson brought a feeling of confidence to the farmers about their "farmers' college." The programs he began in 1891 tripled the enrollment in the agriculture program by 1900. While Curtiss was Wilson's protégé, it was Curtiss's contributions that brought international recognition to the college of agriculture through livestock judging contests.

Curtiss and his family lived in the Farm House for 50 years, from the end of the 19th century to the middle of the 20th century. Because of his lengthy residence in the house, the Farm House became known as the Curtiss House, and for many it remains and always will be the Curtiss House.

7 · *The Final Years of Active Use*

*A*fter Charles Curtiss's death in 1947, Professor Elizabeth Hoyt of the Department of Economics shared the Farm House with two other employees of the college, Dr. Frances (Mary Agnes) Carlin and Beulah McBride. They lived there until the summer of 1948 when the house was reconditioned for use as a "home management house." The concept of home management houses was very similar to the original model farm concept—classroom studies combined with practical work experience. These home management houses flourished on the Iowa State College campus from 1929 until the 1960s when they gradually ceased operations in response to the changing needs of the students. The Farm House only served as a home management house for the 1948–49 school year, but during that time more than 20 young women and two small infants lived there. In 1949 it once again became home to the dean of agriculture. Floyd Andre would be the third and final dean to live in the house.

Dr. Henry Kildee, who was dean of agriculture in 1947, had no intentions of moving to the Farm House after Charles Curtiss's death and was in fact contemplating retirement. Except for Dr. Hoyt's belongings, the house was quite empty. After Charles Curtiss's death, the family's unwanted furniture was sold and the entire first floor was cleared of Charles's possessions. Years later J. C. "Shorty" Schilletter, who was in charge of campus residences, remembered housing was quite tight on campus; he remembered assigning several women to the Farm House, but he was not certain if anyone was then living in the house with Dr. Hoyt. In January 1948, Dr. Frances Carlin and Beulah McBride moved into the Farm House with Dr. Hoyt.

Dr. Carlin was quite happy to move from her small living quarters south of the college and was grateful for the added space of the house and the convenience of living on campus. She was a recent graduate of the doctorate program in food and nutrition at the college and was looking forward to her new position as assistant professor in the same department. Beulah McBride was also beginning a new job at the college as assistant food manager at the Memorial Union. Dr. Hoyt began living at the Curtiss House (Farm House) in 1936 when she rented a bedroom on the second floor of the house from Olive and Charles Curtiss. Her association with them was warm and friendly and the house was as much her home as theirs. While other faculty members who rented rooms in the house saw it as a short-term residence, Elizabeth remained there for 11 years.

Dr. Hoyt began her career at Iowa State College in 1925 after completing her doctorate in economics at Radcliffe College. She accepted a position as associate professor in the Department of Economics and was promoted to full professor two years later. As a young professor, Dr. Hoyt received a Fullbright grant and lectureship in Guatemala and traveled extensively in South America and Africa, observing living conditions in these countries. During her travels Hoyt wrote profusely and passionately, recording first-hand impressions of the problems facing the people in these countries. After one visit to Africa Dr. Hoyt began collecting books for a library she hoped to establish on a return visit to the country. Isabel Matterson, who worked at the college library and was Dr. Hoyt's personal friend, said that she was out to save the world!

Dr. Hoyt taught classes in both the economics and the home management programs and wrote three books based on her lectures: *Consumption of Wealth* (1928), *Consumption in Our Society* (1938), and *American Income and Its Use* (1954). When she retired in 1975, she was honored for her 50 years of service to the college and her research, which formed the basis for the National Consumer Price Index. Dr. Hoyt was the type of person, according to her many friends, who spent her life doing good for others, and it may have been her idea to use the Farm House as a home management house.

The Department of Home Management, which was one of three departments formed in 1929 from the original Department of Household Administration, offered more electives than any other home economics program in the country. It also offered a broad educational program preparing students for work in extension and the social ser-

Dr. Elizabeth Hoyt, ca.
1940s.
*Courtesy Iowa State University
Library/University Archives*

Dr. Frances Carlin, ca.
1940s.
*Courtesy Iowa State University
Library/University Archives*

The kitchen of the Farm House as home management
house, 1948.
Courtesy of Iowa State University Library/University Archives

vices. Dr. Ercel Eppright of Iowa State College wrote in his "Century of Home Economics" essay:

> The Home Management Department at Iowa State College became a center for preparing home management house advisers, for whom there was a large demand because most colleges offering home economics considered living in a home management house a vital part of their curricula.

In an interview for a 1949 article in the *News of Iowa State,* Dr. Paulena Nickell, head of the home management department, stressed the fact that the "houses are *management* houses and not *practice* houses. Occupants have complete responsibility for making their living plans." An essential ingredient for a home management house was a modern kitchen, and remodeling of the Farm House began just as soon as Hoyt, Carlin, and McBride moved from the house at the end of the 1948 spring quarter.

The kitchen, which dated from the 1920s when new cabinets were added for Mrs. Curtiss, was not a large room, and a partitioned-off area where dishes were stored made it seem even smaller. By removing the partition, which ran from the west wall in a semicircle to the south wall, the room was opened to allow for modern cabinets and appliances. The kitchen (with the partition removed) was 13 feet, 6 inches long by 13 feet wide. The east window was shortened to allow for built-in cabinets that lined the east wall and extended halfway along the south wall. Standing in front of the new built-in sink on the east wall you could look directly out of the east window. A small wall shelf was mounted above the stove on the south wall and another one was placed on the west wall to hold small objects. A small drop-leaf table next to the modern refrigerator was the only furniture in the room. The Curtiss bathroom adjacent to the kitchen on the west was converted into a laundry and service room, and both rooms were painted and refloored with linoleum.

Marjorie Garfield, professor of applied art, was in charge of decorating the house. She selected green wool, room size carpets for the first-floor rooms along with wallpaper and furniture to complement the color. An article in the *News of Iowa State* reported on some of the renovations and decorations:

> The entire house was replastered and all but four of the 15 rooms were repapered. [The reported number

of rooms in the house varies depending on whether bathrooms are counted as rooms.] The hallway and advisor's room were repapered with reproductions of old colonial paper....All of the furniture now in the house was chosen from the home management supply of furnishings, with an eye to keeping a harmonious appearance to the interior. Much of the beauty of the old wood in the house was brought out. The beautiful old stairway of solid walnut was rubbed down and refinished.

There were two bathrooms on the second floor; one was located between the two south front bedrooms and the other was the small room in the north kitchen wing. Both of these bathrooms were modernized, and on the first floor, a shower, stool, and sink were added to make a small bathroom in the northeast corner of the room that was once used as the west kitchen and was later used as a bedroom by Charles and Olive Curtiss. On the third floor, the large closet that extended behind the staircase was partitioned to form two separate closets—one opening into the hallway as before and the other opening into the west bedroom. It was during this summer renovation that workers removed the fireplace in the former Curtiss library because it was deemed unsafe to use. The east wall where the fireplace stood was plastered and painted over, leaving only a trace of its location. The fireplace was uncovered and reconstructed in 2006.

In September 1948, the Farm House became one of five home management houses on campus. It was now ready for the fall session and the first group of eager students who were completing their senior year at the college. Marquita Irland, a member of the faculty, was selected advisor for the Farm House home management house and moved into her room there shortly before the students arrived. She was remembered by one student who lived at the house as a "hard taskmaster." Dr. Nickell commented that the "older woman is present in an advisory capacity only," which she said was a vast improvement over the previous practice houses that emphasized perfection and not management experience.

Each graduating senior in the home management program was required to spend six weeks in a home management house taking charge of everyday duties while attending classes. Most amazingly, the duties included caring for a small infant—an orphan provided by and under the supervision of Iowa Children's Services of Des Moines. The women cared for two small infants at the Farm House in 1948–49, baby Maria (Marcia Ann) in the fall and baby Steven Craig

Curtiss in the spring. Marion DeBois Nelson ('49) later wrote, "Our baby was being adopted at the end of our stay to make a happy Christmas for someone."

A typical day began early, before classes started, caring for the baby and planning the meals for the day. Kathy Crowell Knapp ('49) was in charge of preparing meals at the Farm House during the spring Veishea weekend at the college and had to stretch the 70 cents per person a day food budget to feed all the visiting relatives. As she recalled, "I think we mostly reduced the portions and tried to put it on the plate so that it wouldn't appear too skimpy. Appearance and presentation were the watchwords."

The southeast parlor (Curtiss library) as used by the Department of Home Management, 1948. *Back row, left to right:* Marquita Irland, Pat McKee, Mary Lueder Nye, Anita Ohlsen; *front row, left to right:* Peg Ford, Marion DeBois Nelson holding baby Marcia Ann, and Pat Howell Hutchins.
Courtesy of Marion DeBois Nelson

Baby Marcia Ann, 1948.
Courtesy of Marion DeBois Nelson

The southeast parlor (Curtiss library) as home management house, 1948. *Left to right:* Anita Ohlsen, Patricia Howell Hutchins, baby Marcia Ann, Pat McKee, and Mary Lueder Nye.
Courtesy of Iowa State University Library/University Archives

The west parlor of the Farm House as home management house, 1948. *Left to right:* Peg Ford (*seated*), Anita Ohlsen (*on floor*), Mary Lueder Nye, baby Marcia Ann, Marion DeBois Nelson, Patricia Howell Hutchins, and Pat McKee (*back to camera*).
Courtesy of Iowa State University Library/University Archives

Marion DeBois Nelson, who lived at the Farm House management house in the fall of 1948, remembered the Farm House as "beautiful and the atmosphere very homelike." Her roommate was Pearl (Peg) Ford and out of the seven women students in the house at the time, they were the only ones who didn't smoke or drink coffee. Marion listed the duties assigned for the week: assistant housekeeper, housekeeper, assistant cook, cook, manager, assistant baby tender, and baby tender. Each woman took over one duty for an entire week at a time. When it was their job to do the housekeeping, Mary Lueder Nye said she and Pat Howell devised a unique way of polishing the floors by placing dust mop heads on their feet and "skating" across the floors. Mary and Pat were among the last to polish the floors in the Farm House management house before it was transferred back to the agriculture department.

Andre family on the south porch of the Farm House, 1949. *Left to right:* Hazel, Jacqueline, Richard, Alice, and Floyd Andre.
Courtesy of Richard Andre

In the spring of 1949, while the Farm House was still a home management house, a search began for a replacement for Herbert H. Kildee, dean of agriculture, who was retiring from the college. Jacqueline Andre (Schmeal), who was 11 years old that spring, recalled seeing her father, Floyd Andre, come bounding across a vacant lot to their home in Madison, Wisconsin, with the news that he had been appointed dean of the College of Agriculture at Iowa State College. Floyd was then assistant dean of the College of Agriculture at the University of Wisconsin and the assistant director of extension at the college. The dean's position at Iowa State would give him the opportunity to move back to Iowa and, as his daughter Jacqueline wrote, "If anything is outstanding about our father, it was his love of Iowa. He had opportunities to go other places, but he liked Iowa."

Floyd Andre was born in New Sharon, Iowa, on September 13, 1909, where his father owned a general store. According to his younger sister, Vivian, the family owned a farm near New Sharon but it was an investment and the family did not live on it. At the age of 10 Floyd moved from Iowa with his family to Pasadena, California, but Vivian said he "disliked California from the beginning, and each summer returned to New Sharon, Iowa to live with his Aunt Floy and Uncle Ted Sloan and work on their farm." Floyd loved Iowa and farming, and against his father's wishes—he wanted Floyd to attend Cal. Tech.—Floyd moved back to Iowa to attend Iowa State College and to work on his uncle's farm during the summers. He completed his undergraduate degree in 1931 at Iowa State College and earned his doctorate in entomology in 1936. Andre then accepted a position in Washington, D.C. and later returned to the Midwest for a faculty position at the University of Wisconsin at Madison.

Floyd Andre became dean of agriculture at Iowa State College in the summer of 1949 and was assigned the Farm House for his family's residence. It was not a requirement to live at the Farm House as it had been for Charles Curtiss in 1897, but it was still a convenience and an honor to live on the campus. In exchange for the $150-a-month rent which Floyd paid, the college provided all repairs on the house, shoveled the snow from the walks in the winter, and kept the grass mowed in the summer, which Floyd considered a definite bargain. The Andre family moved into the Farm House in August 1949, amid the dust generated by the plasterers and the noise of the carpenters, electricians, and plumbers who were busy at work. Hazel wrote to friends that "Floyd, who had first-hand experience with remodeling two old houses, found it a novel and delightful experience just to kibitz this time."

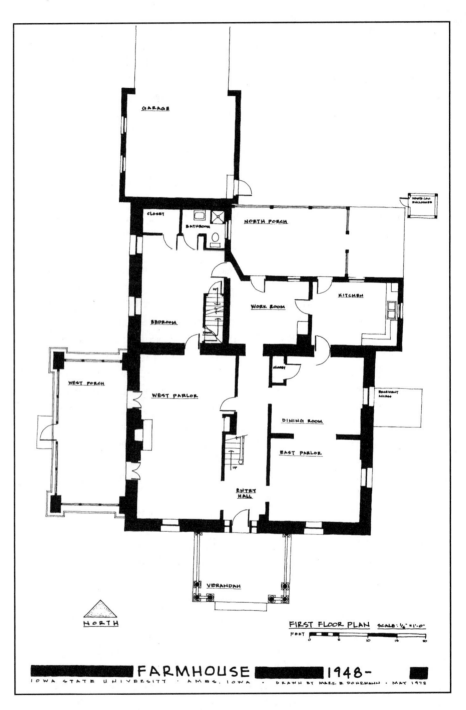

Floor plans of the Farm House, 1948. Drawn by Mark Dohrman, 1972. *Courtesy of Iowa State University Department of Facilities Planning and Management*

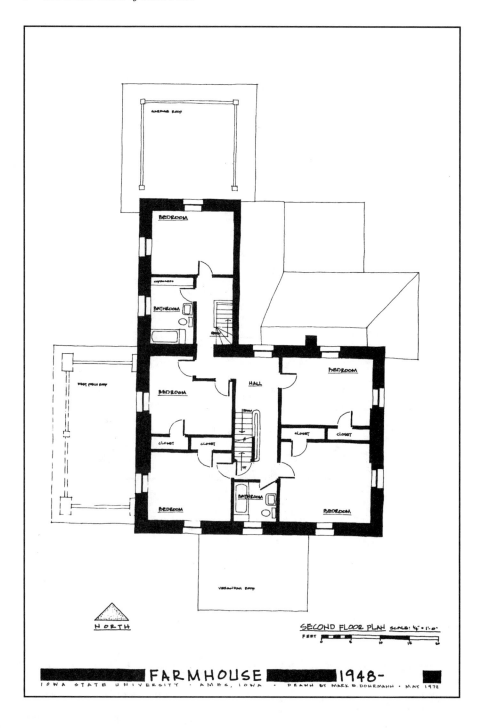

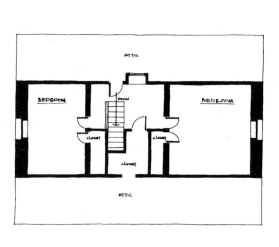

NORTH

THIRD FLOOR PLAN   SCALE: ¼"=1'-0"

FARMHOUSE   1948-

IOWA STATE UNIVERSITY · AMES, IOWA · DRAWN BY MARK B DOHRMANN · MAY 1972

Farm House dining room, 1950s.
Courtesy of Iowa State University Library/University Archives

Floyd Andre in his workshop (the west bedroom) on the third floor of
the Farm House, ca. 1960s.
Courtesy of Avis Andre

Floyd Andre in front of the fireplace (west parlor) in the Farm House,
ca. 1960s.
Courtesy of Iowa State University Library/University Archives

When home management moved from the Farm House, most of
the furniture the department used was moved to other home management houses on campus. However, they left most of the west parlor furniture, the green wool carpets, and the drapes on the first floor.
The Andre family brought with them furniture from their six-room
house in Madison and gradually added antiques to help fill the rooms
at the Farm House.

Floyd converted the third-floor west bedroom to a carpenter's
shop and was excited to find some walnut boards in the basement
which he used for a furniture project. The children used the east
third-floor bedroom as a doll house and storage area. On the second
floor, Hazel and Floyd used the front southwest bedroom, Alice the
southeast room, Jackie the L-shaped west bedroom with large French
windows leading out to the west porch roof, and Richard the end
north bedroom, in the old kitchen ell, with the still functional 1860s
skylight on the east ceiling. Richard was also next to the bathroom
and the back stairway which led down to the room used by his fa-

ther as a study and storage space for his collection of thrips. (Andre's collection of thrips [small insects] is now in the British Museum in London.) The family used the former Curtiss library as a living room and always ate their meals in the adjacent dining room except when the weather permitted dining on the back screened porch.

Hazel Andre was delighted to be living in the Farm House. It was just a short walk from Floyd's office in Curtiss Hall and he often came home for lunch and conversation with Hazel. She and Floyd met as students at Iowa State College and married in 1935 in the formal Horticulture Gardens, which were then located just north of the Farm House. After Hazel graduated in 1933, she worked for President Friley while Floyd finished his doctoral degree. In 1936, Floyd accepted a position with the Bureau of Entomology and Quarantine Service and in 1938 they moved to Washington, D.C., where Floyd worked for the U.S. Department of Agriculture. All three of their children were born while Hazel and Floyd lived in the nation's capital.

Richard Andre revisiting the Farm House basement where he played as a child, ca. 1960s.
Courtesy of Richard Andre

The Andre children—Jacqueline, Alice, and Richard, then 11, eight, and six years old—soon discovered that the college campus was a wonderful place to explore, especially, as Jacqueline later wrote, "in the evening when few people were around. The Christian Petersen pool in the [courtyard of] the Dairy Building was one of our favorite secret spots." Another favorite place to explore was the cellar of the Farm House, which Jacqueline wrote was "always a scary place with its hidden tunnels and soil floor. Our friends thought it was the most special place in the house and always wanted to explore for hidden treasure—or dead bodies." (Heavy black soil compacted by years of heavy footsteps covered the original brick floor, making it appear as if it were a dirt floor. The dirt was removed during the 1970s renovation.) The Andre children attended school with the other campus children from the Platt, Schaefer, Dixon, and Edwards families, riding their bicycles to Welch Junior High southwest of the campus and later, as Jacqueline remembered, "often standing in blizzards in front of Beardshear [Hall] waiting for the bus to take them to [Ames High] school."

Hazel Andre found life at the Farm House definitely lacking in privacy but she accepted it all in good humor. The family's first Christmas letter from the Farm House, dated Christmas 1949, reflected on the "disadvantages of being housed so publicly." Hazel wrote,

> She learned the hard way not to step outside the house unless decently attired. One morning this fall—before she [Hazel] had dressed herself and hair properly for the day—she dashed out on the porch to put a letter in the slot and found 20 college boys and their botany teacher studying the vine that grows up one side of the porch. You can see her days of hanging up the wash in sloppy slacks are over.

Still, Hazel was always happy to show visitors around the Farm House and enjoyed sharing the history of the house with them.

The Andre family home was always open to visitors at the college, and it was not unusual for Floyd to bring home a last-minute guest for lunch or for a hastily arranged dinner party. Hazel was prepared for these occasions with the help of a large freezer on the back screened porch which, according to Jacqueline, was filled with "mile high pies and tarts ready for anyone who might drop in at the last minute." At these dinner parties, Floyd took great delight in serving domestic Iowa soybeans to his guests, but all his children could think about was the hours spent shelling the soybeans and their blistered thumbs.

At a 1953 luncheon at the Farm House, Hazel and Floyd entertained the former secretary of agriculture and vice-president of the United States, Henry Wallace. Henry was the grandson of Henry "Uncle Henry" Wallace who himself frequently dined at the Farm House as a guest of James "Tama Jim" Wilson in the 1890s. Hazel wrote to a friend, "He's [Henry Wallace] a most interesting conversationalist, though I was a little pushed to keep up with his pure genetics."

In 1955 Hazel and Floyd Andre were confronted with the devastating news that she was suffering from pancreatic cancer. Hazel wrote that "I would rather live 42 full, rich years than twice that long in dull tempo....I have no regrets....My life has been rich and full and I have loved every minute of it." During her last year, she spent her days at home at the Farm House with her family. Jacqueline Andre (Schmeal) wrote that her "Mother lived all but her last two weeks at the Farm House—cooking until she couldn't and visiting with all of her friends even when her strength was gone." Carl Hamilton, a close friend of the family, encouraged Hazel to write about her personal thoughts during that last year. Hazel's article entitled "My Last Wonderful Days" was first published in the July 1956 issue of the *Farm Journal,* three months after her death in April 1965. Even today, the article remains an inspiration to all who read it.

After Hazel's death, the children assisted with the cooking and Mrs. Minear continued to help at the house as she had done for Hazel. Later, to help with the household duties, Floyd hired students from the college who also roomed with the family at the Farm House. Floyd always kept the family busy. On weekends they worked on the farm that Hazel and Floyd purchased in Hamilton County; and Christmas holidays became the time for family trips to Florida, Texas, or Mexico. Jacqueline was the first to leave home. She enrolled at Iowa State College in 1956 and moved into a student dormitory on the campus. Alice Andre decided on the nursing program at the University of Iowa and left for classes in 1959. With Richard's sisters in college, Floyd remarked in his 1959 Christmas greeting that "...Ellen Dihlmann and Norma Refle [resident student housekeepers] keep him [Richard] inspired study wise, with good food."

On the 100th anniversary of the 1859 Fourth of July picnic to celebrate the location of the agriculture college in Story County, Iowa State College once again changed its name, this time to Iowa State University of Science and Technology. The name change reflected the growth of the college and its prominence in the international agricultural scene. The same year, Floyd Andre represented the university when Premier Khrushchev of the former Soviet Union visited Iowa. Floyd wrote, "If you watched the television news reels during Mr. K's visit to Iowa, you may have seen Father [Floyd] presenting the Premier with a plastic pig at the nutrition farm. He also rode from Coon Rapids to Ames with the Mr. K talking about students, scholarships, money, corn and the Soviet."

In the 1960s Floyd began traveling to South America on behalf of the university as administrative advisor for the university's AID (Agency for International Development) contracts. In November 1961, Floyd wrote from Argentina, "Visited a 60,000 acre ranch today. Get invited to more places than I can get to since I need to keep up-to-date on reports. *Ale enemates.* Go to Brazil next week." In addition to his role as advisor for the AID contracts, Andre assisted with agricultural programs in Mexico, Argentina, Brazil, Uruguay, Peru, and Paraguay.

Floyd developed an interest in flying, since he was doing so much of it, and began flying lessons in the early 1960s. His enthusiasm for flying was not diminished by injuries he suffered in an airplane accident in Atlantic, Iowa, in October 1962, when the university airplane crashed on takeoff. Both Floyd Andre and another passenger, Avis Lovell (the future Mrs. Andre), broke their backs in the accident. Avis recovered faster than Floyd, who wore a back brace for a year. Together, Avis and Floyd completed flight ground school and Floyd went on to get a pilot's license in 1967. Later, they purchased their own plane and used it to travel back and forth from their farm to Ames.

The Farm House was 100 years old in 1961. No grand celebration marked the occasion and, at the house, little notice was taken of the significance of the year. The Farm House, however, was developing problems which were particularly obvious in the second-floor southwest bedroom. The wooden beam across the center of the parlor directly below this bedroom sagged, as did the floor that it supported. Mrs. Minear, Floyd's housekeeper, became so concerned about the one-inch separation between the north wall of the room and the floor that one day while Floyd was on a trip, she removed his furniture and belongings from the room and placed them all in another room without telling him. Floyd was greatly surprised when he arrived home from his trip to find his bedroom empty! (The beam was not replaced until the 1970 restoration.)

Other problems continued to develop with the house. The roof

Farm House in the winter, ca. 1960s.
Courtesy of Iowa State University Library/University Archives

sprung numerous leaks and water began running down the third-floor walls, damaging the plaster. The heating system was erratic and Floyd said that, during the cold months, the kitchen was often just above freezing—and that was the highest temperature it reached during the day. The physical plant employees at the university maintained the house and always took special care to get things fixed for Floyd, although the Farm House stood in line for repair funds just like any other building on campus. Floyd said his family didn't seem to notice all the problems because the Farm House was home to them.

The Farm House underwent close scrutiny in the early 1960s as a result of the national interest in identifying historically significant sites and buildings in preparation for the nation's bicentennial celebration in 1976. The U.S. Department of the Interior's 1960 survey of historic sites identified the Farm House as nationally significant because of two of its former residents—Seaman Knapp and James "Tama Jim" Wilson. Stewart Udall, Secretary of the Interior, recommended that the Farm House be declared a National Historic Landmark, which he said is "a unique status accorded limited numbers of properties meeting the stringent criteria of national significance." Dr. James H. Hilton, president of the university, signed an official application in 1964 asking for a certificate and plaque designating the Farm House a National Historic Landmark. The Department of the Interior dubbed it the "Knapp-Wilson House," but Dr. Hilton insisted that it be officially called the "Farm House."

On Friday, June 4, 1965, at 4 P.M., a special ceremony took place at the Farm House. There, Merrill J. Mattes, acting resource studies advisor for the U.S. Department of the Interior, presented the plaque to President James H. Hilton and Floyd Andre on behalf of the Secretary of the Interior. The event was planned to coincide with Alumni Days at the university and Dean Floyd Andre opened the ceremony with a short history of the Farm House. The bronze plaque, later placed on

Floyd Andre at his farm in Hamilton County, Iowa, ca. 1960s.
Courtesy of Avis Andre

Merril J. Mattes (*left*) and Floyd Andre at the ceremony at Farm House designating it a National Historic Landmark, June 4, 1965.
Courtesy of Iowa State University Library/University Archives

a small boulder that sits at the bottom of the front steps to the Farm House, reads:

> The Farm House has been designated a Registered National Historic Landmark under the Provisions of the Historic Sites Act of August 21, 1935. This site possesses exceptional value in commemorating and illustrating the history of the United States. U.S. Department of the Interior National Park Service. 1965

Although the ceremony was brief, it was significant because as a National Historic Landmark, the Farm House would later become eligible for federal funds during its restoration in the 1970s.

The last of the Andre children moved from the Farm House in 1966 when Richard graduated from Iowa State and left for graduate school. Floyd's carpentry projects, his work at the university, frequent trips hunting for thrips, and visits to his children and their growing families kept him occupied. Holiday greetings to friends in 1969 included the usual third-person account of the year:

> FA [Floyd Andre] keeps busy and is especially proud of 3,000 undergraduates, 600 graduate students and the outstanding work of the College of Agriculture staff for the benefit of Iowa's agricultural economy and people. As you can see [referring to a photograph of his farm on the front of the greeting]...he still relaxes at the farm in Hamilton County.

The first dean of agriculture, James "Tama Jim" Wilson, would have been astounded at the number of students enrolled in the agriculture programs in 1969 and would have found great satisfaction in his own work, which essentially changed the course of the agriculture program at the university.

In the fall of 1969, Andre began construction on a new home for himself and his intended bride, Avis Lovell. The new home was south of campus on Ashmore Circle. Andre planned to move from the Farm House by summer. The last official function hosted by Dean Floyd Andre at the Farm House was a reception for the faculty members of the College of Agriculture in December 1969. The Farm House stood vacant after Andre moved out in July 1970. He and Avis were married on November 12, 1970, and took an extended trip to Malaysia and New Zealand before settling into their new home.

Before Andre moved from the Farm House, he began a campaign to save the house from possible demolition. He knew that its status as a National Historic Landmark did not guarantee its continuance. Andre recognized (as had Charles Curtiss) that the Farm House was a very important part of the heritage of the university. But not everyone agreed. The struggle to preserve the Farm House was just beginning.

8 · Restoration and Museum

*A*fter 110 years of continual use, there were no immediate plans for another tenant after Andre moved out in the summer of 1970. Some believed the Farm House had outlived its usefulness on campus and there was talk of just bulldozing the century-old house, since it needed substantial repairs, to make room for a modern classroom building. For the first time in its long history of service to the college, the Farm House stood empty, waiting for a decision as to its fate.

Andre and the dean of the Department of Home Economics, Helen LeBaron, were in favor of preserving the Farm House as a "heritage house." They wrote to John Pace and William Whitman on May 14, 1970, urging that an advisory committee be formed with the specific purpose of developing a plan for furnishing each room of the house and establishing guidelines for soliciting gifts and specific items needed for the house. They also recommended that the committee be made up of faculty members from the Colleges of Agriculture and Home Economics "with particular interest in the project and knowledgeable of period furnishings and equipment." Both deans also pledged their departments' commitment to be responsible for the management of the Farm House if it became a heritage house.

John Pace, head of the Office of Space and Schedules, and William Whitman, director of the physical plant at the university, quickly endorsed Andre and LeBaron's proposal and sent a memo to Iowa State president W. Robert Parks asking if he concurred with the proposal and if so to "indicate the same to the good Deans."

President Parks, known for his contributions to Iowa State's cul-

---

This chapter is adapted in part from an article commissioned by the University Museums and written by Debra Steilen, former curator of the Farm House Museum.

tural climate, responded immediately by appointing Carl Hamilton, vice president of information and development at the university, as chair of a committee whose mission was the renovation of the Farm House. Hamilton selected committee members who represented areas directly concerned with renovation and preservation: Neva Petersen, professor of applied art; Wesley Shank, professor of architecture; and Robert Harvey, professor of landscape architecture. Lawton Patten, professor of architecture, joined the committee in 1973.

The first meeting of the Farm House committee took place on April 1, 1971. Hamilton, Petersen, Shank, and Harvey began by establishing goals for the project: the integrity of the house would be maintained and furnished in a manner to make the structure into a totally useful facility. As Hamilton later explained, the committee decided that there would be a "cut-off" date of 1910-12 for the rehabilitation and furnishing of the house. They were not planning to make it any particular period but instead to "reflect the living conditions and life style that prevailed throughout the total occupation." The date was determined by the exterior of the house, which was stuccoed in 1910-12 to stabilize the outside walls of the house. To remove the stucco and return the exterior of the house to an earlier period would destroy the soft red bricks beneath the stucco. Wesley Shank agreed to gather information on the Farm House from the university archives to assist with the restoration project.

On April 20, 1971, the committee members met for the first time at the Farm House. They invited Dean Floyd Andre to join them on an inspection tour of the house with John Pace, Charles DeKovic, and Rupert Kenyon from the university's physical plant. Everyone was shocked and dismayed with the obvious deterioration of the house and the enormous task ahead of them. Most of the damage to the interior of the house was due to moisture seeping through the roof, walls, doors and windows. The ceiling in the west parlor was sagging across the center. The worst damage was on the third floor where water had loosened the plaster on the ceilings. In one room the moisture had gone through to the floor below. The committee agreed that fixing the roof was the first priority and work on the interior could not begin until the house was weatherproofed.

The apparently simple matter of roofing the house turned out not to be so simple. The work included repairing and rebuilding portions of the roof structure, rebuilding the built-in gutters, installing sheet metal flashing, reroofing all the sloping roofs with wood shingles, and rebuilding the upper portion of the east chimneys. The estimated cost to complete the work was $9,000. Wesley Shank disagreed with the decision to reroof with wood shingles, which he said were costly and a fire hazard. Although the original shingles were oak and walnut, Shank believed that the asbestos shingles dated from around 1910-12 when the house was reroofed. He recommended using a fire-rated shingle of a light gray color. Wood shingles won in the end. Unfortunately, during the reroofing process the two skylights installed in 1867 by A. J. Graves were removed because they were believed, at the time, to be a 20th-century addition. (Information on the skylights was uncovered during research for this book and was chronicled in the *College Farm Journal.*)

In April 1972, Carl Hamilton received a letter from Dr. Adrian Anderson, state historical preservation officer of the Division of Historic Preservation, confirming that the Farm House, as a National Historic Landmark, was eligible for federal funds for renovations. It was good news to Hamilton since the university had so far paid all the costs of the work on the Farm House. He immediately urged William Whitman and the Farm House committee to determine what else needed to be done since the house was eligible for federal funds.

The committee began work on a detailed preservation plan for the Farm House. Wesley Shank advised the committee to make certain everything that was needed was included in the plan. He cautioned, "We cannot piecemeal suggest a little bit of work every year as a separate program. Funds will be awarded for only one program, so this must be complete." The first draft was ready May 23, 1972. Hamilton wrote to Wesley Shank, "Your start on the Farm House draft sounds good to me....We might emphasize a little more strongly our hope that there would be furnishings which might reflect living conditions and life styles as they existed when the house was first occupied." The preservation plan defined the scope of the project and the project budget. It also clarified who would direct the restoration—the Farm House committee—and who would do the actual work—Iowa State University's physical plant.

Charles DeKovic, university architect, directed the physical plant's efforts. He provided the proposed work plan and budget estimate for the renovation. The exterior work included removing the 1926 garage and foundation, patching the stucco where the garage was attached to the house, and repairing or replacing all painted wood surfaces. Inside the house, shoring up sagging floors and patching plaster would be finished first before repainting woodwork, sanding and refinishing floors, removing wallpaper and repapering.

The plan also called for restoring the second-floor front bathroom, re-modeling the rear bathroom and refinishing the west parlor, library, and dining room on the first floor. The mechanical and electrical work included converting the steam heating system to a hot-water heating system and adding air conditioning, a fire alarm system, and security system. DeKovic estimated the entire project would cost $10,000. The budget also included $15,000 for furnishings and an-other $3,000 for landscaping.

It took almost a year to finish the roofing project and complete the preservation plan for the house. The final budget was increased to $34,870 with the committee asking the federal government for one half of that amount in matching funds. The revised budget estimate included $19,870 for renovation, $12,000 for furnishings and $3,000

The original north door from the west kitchen, un-covered during restoration. *All photographs in Chapter 8 are courtesy of the Farm House Museum Archives*

The west parlor after the wood had been stripped.

for landscaping. (As it turned out, all the furniture and money for furnishings were donated to the project.) The Department of the Interior approved the grant for a three-year period beginning June 11, 1973. All work covered by the grant would have to be completed by June 10, 1976.

DeKovic initially planned to have the first phase of the renovation completed by June 30, 1973. However, work on the outside of the house did not go as planned. Each step in the process raised new questions. The garage was removed, revealing the old doorway on the north wall of the 1860s kitchen bricked in with soft, crumbling red bricks. The Farm House committee decided to leave the doorway and the bricks in place and restucco the area on the exterior of the house. The bricks can now be viewed by opening the door inside the room.

Once the garage was gone, work on the exterior painted wood surfaces began. There were 25 windows to repair and paint, four exterior doors, and three porches. All of these areas were first stripped of old paint and new wood was substituted where the original wood was decaying. Wood from the old horticulture farm house replaced the ceiling in the west screen porch. Before any tinted paint was applied, all the wood surfaces were first given a primer coat and two coats of off-white paint. The north screened porch was painted light gray to blend in with the stucco on the main part of the house. Window screens were painted black and porch floors were painted battleship gray in keeping with traditional colors from the 1910-12 era.

While physical plant employees were hard at work on the exterior of the Farm House, an interested public was eagerly donating (and in some cases threatening to donate) furnishings to complete the project. By the fall of 1972, offerings included two Victorian walnut chairs, a handmade sofa and an old-fashioned dress form which Hamilton described as going back to "the days when there was a great deal above and below but not much in the middle of a woman's figure."

Iowa State University's Twenty-five Year Club members also wanted to help. The club's president, Dr. Mack Emmerson, wrote to Hamilton: "The members of the I.S.U. Twenty-five Year Club increase year by year, but the recollections of important events at the turn of the century become less and less....If we can help before it is too late, call on us."

Carl Hamilton advised against placing any antiques in the Farm House before the entire house was repaired. The best solution was offered by John Pace, director of Office of Space and Schedules at the university. He informed Hamilton and DeKovic that Farm House furniture could be stored in Friley Hall in the care of the Department of Residence although they were not willing to guarantee that the antiques would not be damaged or lost. Nevertheless the Farm House committee thought this was a reasonable solution to its immediate problem. In view of the fact that furniture was already arriving and would continue to arrive, Hamilton decided to open an account with the Alumni Achievement Fund for donations to assist with the costs of transportation and other minor expenses. In April 1973, he wrote, "We have no deposits to report as yet," but he was hopeful.

Hamilton wrote to the committee in June and again in August 1973, urging them to set up a schedule for the completion of the interior rooms of the house. He praised them for their herculean efforts saying, "I know that I am asking a good deal of you people on this whole matter, and I am going to call this to the attention of your respective department chairmen so that it may be taken into account."

It took until February 1974 to complete a preliminary set of drawings for the renovation of the interior of the house. Craig Roloff, interior designer, sent copies of the drawings to Carl Hamilton and Elizabeth Foxley, architectural historian of the State Historic Preservation Program, asking for approval of the room-by-room renovation plan. The Farm House committee approved minor changes to the drawings: closets that had wallpaper in excellent condition should be left alone, oil-base paint was recommended for use in the utility and east kitchen areas, and a request was made that the fire and detection systems be connected to an alarm on the exterior of the building in lieu of being tied into the city system.

Repairs on the exterior of the house dragged on into early 1974. The west porch roof needed extensive work. The top decorative wood railing was weak and decaying and had to be entirely replaced. Professor Shank kept a close watch on the work. For example, he objected to the balusters proposed for the porch roof because they were too different from the original ones. Alternative balusters met with his approval. The overall landscaping project, except for the reseeding of the lawn where the garage once stood, came to a halt while Professor Harvey, who was in charge of the project, was away in England.

The interior plan was approved in February 1974, and the physical plant began working inside the house on February 11. On the third floor they removed the plaster and lath on all the walls and what was left of the ceiling. The baseboards, doors, and window trim were removed, stripped of paint, and replaced. In some areas new wood replaced the rotting baseboard and trim. The flooring was patched by using boards from the adjacent closets.

Gypsum board replaced the wood lath on the ceilings and walls. A plaster coating was used to prepare the boards for painting. Replacing the original wood lath and plaster with gypsum board raised the question of "honesty" in restoration. Both Petersen and Shank believed that "so long as the finished effect or surface is in harmony with the desired plan, and it is economical, then modern materials as well as techniques are satisfactorily used in restoration." Shank also commented that as long as the substituted materials are not passed off as original, the result is both an honest and economical solution.

On the second floor, the southwest bedroom floor sagged a full inch, which caused the interior wall to separate from the floor. To stabilize the floor and the ceiling below, the original walnut support

[Above Left] A third-floor view of the hallway and the west bedroom from the east bedroom during restoration. [Left] The same view after the walls were replaced. [Above] The stairway to the third floor during restoration.

A cracked support beam removed from the west parlor ceiling.

beam, which had cracked, was removed and a steel beam was used. A slight shadow across the room now marks the location of the new beam.

The committee believed the bathroom between the two front bedrooms on the second floor had to go since it was thought to have been installed during the 1920s. Research has since shown that this bathroom was originally installed in 1896 by James "Tama Jim" Wilson. The bathroom fixtures and the walls enclosing the area were removed. The floor was patched to match the oak tongue-and-groove flooring in the hallway. The area is now used as a sitting area as it might have been when the house was first built. It was decided to restore the back north bathroom by using antique fixtures selected by the committee. It would not, however, be a functioning bathroom. (These bathroom fixtures were removed in the 1990s following a decision to return the room to a bedroom, which was its original use.)

Of primary concern on the first level was the sagging floor in the main hallway. Floor joists were replaced and support jack posts were placed under the floor to hold it in position. Support jack posts were also placed under the main rooms on the first floor. The supports stabilized the floor but did not straighten them. The floors still sag noticeably, which can be disturbing to visitors. In 1991 additional

The second-floor hallway, looking south. The bathroom, exposed during restoration, was later removed.

supports were added under the floors—this time to museum-weight standards—to accommodate the large number of people attending museum events.

Once the floors were stabilized, work began on the walls and ceilings. All the old wallpaper was stripped from the rooms. This loosened the original plaster from the walls and ceilings and required

The first-floor hallway and stairway looking toward the front (south) entry door.

time-consuming patching. All the woodwork was scraped and the loose paint was removed. A primer was applied but it did not adhere so eventually the woodwork was stripped down to the bare wood. Some of the wood was beautiful walnut or cherry, but most of it was a combination of woods. The committee decided to repaint all the woodwork except the walnut and cherry, which was refinished to bring out the natural beauty of the wood grain.

In August 1974, Hamilton informed the committee that work was going slowly. He said it was "taking the electricians most of the summer to do all of their work on lighting and security measures that are being installed. Now the follow-up people are in healing up the grievous wounds that were left by the electricians." Major cracks appeared in the ceiling after the electrical work was finished. Simply patching the plaster did not cover the badly scarred walls and ceilings. Sheetrock was installed on the ceilings of the dining room, west parlor, original kitchen, and the south bedrooms on the second floor to cover the huge cracks. Eventually, plasterboard was also installed in the ceilings in the east library, entry hall, and the north bedrooms on the second floor.

While the work was continuing on the inside repairs, Neva Petersen began deciding on the wallpapers and furnishings needed throughout the house. Hamilton reported, "Some really big news....Professor Petersen is taking a leave of absence without pay to work on the Farm House. This is her contribution." Petersen retired before the project was completed but continued to volunteer her time. Emelda Kunau and Virginia Denisen agreed to serve with Neva on a subcommittee of the Farm House committee to help with decisions on finishing touches for the interior of the house. To complicate the work of determining furnishings, colors, wallpapers, and paints, there was only one known pre-1910 photograph of the interior of the house. That photo was taken of the Curtiss library in 1907 and it was in black and white. There were few reference books to go by and countless decisions had to be made. Some were clear-cut; others were judgment calls made by Petersen or others on the committee.

Neva was also interested in restoring the fireplace in Dean Curtiss's library, which had been removed in 1948, and she began an investigation into the possibility of rebuilding it. Craig Roloff, project coordinator, wrote to Petersen that he inspected the southeast chimney used by the original fireplace and found a "clear drop within the chimney from the roof to approximately two feet below the first floor....The chimney has either been sealed off or it changes direction....In the basement the fireplace foundation and cleanout structure appears to be very similar to that of the living room fireplace." He suggested that the fireplace should be researched and if it was to be restored, it should be done before the floors were refinished. Lynette Pohlman, then a graduate student in interior design who worked on the Farm House project with Neva, interviewed the workman who removed the fireplace in 1948. He remembered it as a small fireplace with a redbrick face and a shallow hearth. The chimney above the bricks was wallpapered up to the ceiling. Petersen eventually rejected Roloff's proposed plan for the fireplace, saying it was too large and cumbersome. Funding for the fireplace was not in the original proposal, so it was dropped pending further research.

At each step of the way, expenses for the renovation continued to climb. In the cellar a new outside door was installed on the east wall at the bottom of the stairway entrance. The door was constructed according to Petersen's specifications. Also, the brick support walls leading down the stairway were rebuilt.

In the northwest original kitchen, Petersen insisted that all the paint be removed from the wainscoting and that the wood be refinished, not repainted, to appear as it would have when it was originally installed in the 1860s. To their dismay, the workers found 14 layers of paint covering the original wood surface. Petersen also decided the kitchen walls should be painted with old-fashioned white milkpaint: the painting wasn't finished until after the house was opened to the public.

Neva's quest for historically accurate wallpaper was frustrating. Reproductions of wallpaper used by wealthy homeowners in the East at the turn of the century were readily available. Few examples existed from the average Midwest home in the same time period. Other than the 1907 photo of the library, there were no records of the wall-

Workers put finishing touches on the west original kitchen area after removing 14 layers of paint from the wainscoting.

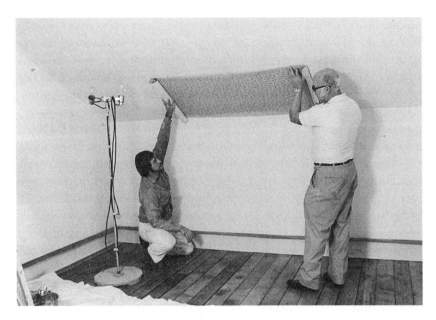

Skip Spring and Bill Hockman prepare to wallpaper walls, 1975.

paper used at the Farm House prior to the 1948 renovation. The layers of wallpaper taken from the walls could not be accurately dated.

Neva turned to the wallpaper firm of Brunswick and Fils, Inc., of New York City, which specialized in reproducing period wallpaper. She was overwhelmed with wallpaper samples sent for her approval. Neva had the unenviable, painstaking task of choosing wallpaper for each room. She decided to experiment. She would take several wallpaper samples at a time, pin them up on the walls in the various rooms and study their effect. Neva solicited opinions from the workers, other committee members, and the occasional visitor to the house. But the final selection rested with Neva. She insisted on authentic reproductions but admitted that she was forced to compromise on the second-floor back north bedroom, bath, and hallway in order to finish the rooms for the scheduled July 1976 public opening. The actual installation of the wallpaper did not begin until early in January 1976.

Another problem arose regarding how people were going to get across the front lawn and into the Farm House. There was only one small sidewalk, which ran from the front steps of the house around to the west porch. There were also stepping stone walks on the southeast and west sides of the house, neither of which was inviting or could accommodate the hoped for number of visitors to the house.

An alternative circular walk was proposed for the front, which would lead to the sidewalk in front of Ross Hall. It would have required a redesign of the west sidewalk intersection and the idea was dropped in favor of a straight brick walk running from the front porch of the house directly to the sidewalk that led to Knoll Road.

The question of illuminating the interior of the house also arose. Should modern fixtures be installed or should the lighting be kept low as it would have been prior to 1910? Here again, the committee was concerned with historical accuracy. Wesley Shank summarized the committee's thoughts on the subject: "Historical authenticity would be best served by using whatever means of lighting were actually used historically....Since the date of the house is to be circa 1910, appropriate electric lighting fixtures, table lamps, and floor lamps will probably be appropriate to the decorating schemes for most rooms." To accommodate visitors to the house, small torch-type floor lamps were purchased and gradually replaced with authentic lighting fixtures as funds became available.

Work continued on the house during the hot summer of 1975. In August, while Neva Petersen was vacationing, volunteers and stu-

[LEFT] Carl Hamilton helps move items into the Farm House, 1975. [RIGHT] Neva Petersen's first view of the donated furniture stored temporarily in the west parlor.

dents pitched in to help move all the donated antique furniture from Friley Hall to the Farm House. The furniture was piled in the west parlor waiting Neva's return. Her first view of the parlor filled with a jumble of items took her breath away. She later commented that it reminded her of the first viewing of "King Tut's tomb." For several days volunteers endured the heat and stairs as they "huffed and puffed" while moving the furniture according to Neva's directions.

In January 1976, Craig Roloff wrote to Neva saying, "Now that our personnel are beginning to install wallpaper…our men are rather uncomfortable about the aspect of having to move the furniture around in the Farm House." He asked Neva to make some of her people available to move and cover furniture as the workers tackled the remaining rooms.

To further jeopardize the completion date of the renovation, all the radiators had been removed for painting and were being returned one at a time. First a room was wallpapered, then the freshly painted radiator was reinstalled. The paint and glass services personnel assured Roloff that they could wallpaper around the radiators so Neva requested that all the radiators be reinstalled at once so she could finish arranging the furniture in the house.

By May 1976 the complex renovation and preservation of the Farm House were almost finished. The hoped-for air conditioning system and new heat plant did not materialize due to lack of funding but the security system was in place, as were smoke detectors in each room. The landscaping of the lawn was put on further hold due to disagreements over exactly what should be planted.

Everyone involved with the project began to look forward to the official opening, especially Craig Roloff, the physical plant's interior designer and the Farm House project manager. Roloff was the one who made almost daily visits to the Farm House during the entire renovation process, checking on work and seeing that everything was going as planned. Roloff wrote to Carl Hamilton in early April 1976 saying that he hoped the project would be fully completed by Veishea (May 6-8) or by July 1, 1976. He was also concerned that June 11, 1976, was the official end of the three-year federal grant period.

The costs for the project, originally estimated at $34,870, continued to increase as the basement-to-roof renovation took place. In 1974 Roloff revised the project budget to $59,584 for additional work on the heating and electrical systems. Even this estimate was low compared to the final total expended: $120,414. In addition to the federal grant from the Department of the Interior, the university as early as 1973 appealed to its extensive public for donations to help pay for restoring and furnishing the house. The project was widely publicized through a university bulletin which went to 70,000 alumni, parents, and friends. Several alumni classes took the Farm House as their special project and contributed financial support for renovation and furnishings.

Work continued on the house even as it was opened to the public. Last minute details such as curtain rods for lace curtains on the first floor, a dehumidifier in the basement, and final coats of paint in the original kitchen were in place by August 1976.

Carl Hamilton praised everyone's efforts on behalf of the Farm House project. Hamilton wrote:

> Special thanks is...due the Farm House committee which guided the restoration project, and to many of the skilled craftsmen from Physical Plant whose careful work is clearly evident throughout the house. But especial appreciation must go to Miss Neva Petersen, who though officially retired, devoted herself to this effort and contributed time, resources, expertise and patience in really large quantities. To her must go much credit for the warm words of approval which Farm House is receiving from visitors.

In a June 28, 1976, memo to "All Parties Interested in or Concerned with the Farm House" Carl Hamilton addressed the future care and maintenance of the Farm House. He wrote, "The operation of the Farm House should become a function of the Iowa State Center, operating essentially as an adjunct of the Brunnier Gallery....Custodial functions should now become a part of the regular Physical Plant operation." Lynette Pohlman, who had since accepted a position at the Brunnier Gallery, said that, at the time, no one wanted to take on the responsibility for the Farm House. Hamilton's recommendation was based on his confidence in Pohlman's abilities and her dedication to the Farm House project. Neva, he wrote, needed to get on with the business of cataloging the gifts received for the house and responding "as she wishes or sees fit to any requests from groups or organizations which wish special tours or programs on the general subject of Farm House."

Neva actually began showing friends around the Farm House months before its official opening. Unofficially, the women of the "Book and Basket Club of Ames" received the first tour of the house conducted by Neva Petersen and Lynette Pohlman in April 1976. Neva later commented that she talked about the Farm House to everyone and anyone who would listen. Whenever Neva could convince friends to visit the house she would walk them through, room by room, pointing out significant pieces of furniture or historic details about the house. Sometimes when Neva brought friends through the house, the workers were there wallpapering or making last minute finishing touches. But they never seemed to mind the intrusions and, in fact, enjoyed sharing stories about the work they were doing.

The Farm House formally opened its doors to the public on the nation's bicentennial, July 4, 1976. The city of Ames celebrated with a huge parade through downtown. Neva placed a U.S. flag in the holder on the Farm House front porch to celebrate the holiday and to let people know the house was open. Following Neva's tradition, the flag continues to be displayed whenever the house is open to the public.

Neva Petersen (*extreme left*) and Lynette Pohlman (*extreme right*) give the first tour of the Farm House to the Ames Book and Basket Club, 1976.

After the initial grand opening of the Farm House, Neva continued to open the house on Sunday afternoons from 2 to 4 P.M. Neva remembered hurrying home from church, grabbing a bite to eat and going to the Farm House to greet visitors, Sunday after Sunday. Lynette Pohlman was there to help Neva and together they kept the house open on Sundays for the next two years.

In 1977 several hundred interested individuals responded to an invitation from the Brunnier Gallery staff to form a support group, "Friends of the Brunnier and Farm House." Volunteers from the Friends group took on the responsibility of greeting guests at the Sunday afternoon open hours at the Farm House while Neva provided an afternoon tour to visitors. Gradually the staff of the Brunnier Gallery began to assist with the Sunday tours and programs.

On October 17, 1979, Carl Hamilton sent a final report on the Farm House project to Adrian Anderson, Iowa's State Historical Preservation Officer. Hamilton concluded his report to Anderson by saying that 22,000 visitors had toured the Farm House since its opening in 1976. It was unfortunate that Dean Floyd Andre died in 1972

Finally a sign! It was donated by Friends of University Museums. *Left to right:* Ruth Smith, Midge Sanders, and Joan Kluge, 1989.

before the project was completed. But Dean Helen LeBaron Hilton visited the house after it was renovated and continued to be an active supporter of the Farm House Museum until her death in 1993.

Volunteers continued to fund and provide the programming for the Farm House Museum until 1983, when the university assumed financial responsibility. In 1969 Deans Andre and Hilton urged that a curator be hired for the museum once it was renovated. The Brunnier Gallery director was finally able to hire the first paid employees for the Farm House in 1983—a curator, Debra Steilen, and student staff who maintained regular museum hours. Steilen served as curator until she resigned in 1986. University Museums director, Lynette Pohlman, then appointed Mary Atherly as curator.

In 1991 the Farm House Museum celebrated its fifteenth year as a museum. Plans for the celebration nearly came to a halt in January of that year with the discovery of a two-inch gap between the floor and walls in the main hallway of the first floor. A similar gap existed

Farm House Museum. The flag on the porch signifies it is open to the public.

Carl Hamilton, Neva Petersen (*center*), and Lynette Pohlman at the 10th
anniversary celebration of the Farm House Museum opening, 1986.

Members of the Farm House Preservation Committee and University Museums staff, 1991. *Left to right:* Wesley Shank; Ray Bentor, information specialist; Mary Atherly, curator; Carl Hamilton; Lynette Pohlman, director; Neva Petersen.

along the west wall in the dining room. Alarmed that the floor supports might be sinking, Atherly requested an immediate inspection of the floors by the university's physical plant staff.

The physical plant staff hired Paul Rietz, a structural engineer, to examine the museum's first floor beams and support system. Rietz discovered that the floors were in danger of collapsing without additional supports so he ordered that the museum be closed to the public. Because the house was already closed for its January-through-March winter schedule, the staff thought they had three months to get the floor supports fixed to meet their scheduled reopening in April. As circumstances dictated, however, the house would remain closed until the Fourth of July.

Rietz insisted that floor supports also be extended under the two wood-framed rooms that had been added in 1886 and were now used as a kitchen and entry room. These rooms had a shallow, eighteen-inch-high crawl space beneath them. A large hole in the north foundation wall of the main house was the only entry to this crawl space. Years earlier, plumbing and electrical lines for the northeast kitchen had been extended under these rooms through the wall opening and across the crawl space.

Because the house was a National Historic Landmark and this area had never been excavated, it was important that it be done by professional archaeologists and that any historic artifacts be documented. They needed to make sure nothing of historical value had

[LEFT] Fourth of July community celebration at the Farm House Museum, 1993.

been dropped or discarded in this area before the rooms were added. The curator received approval for an emergency Historical Resource Development Program grant from the State Historical Society of Iowa for both the excavation and the building of the support system.

In May 1991, a team of archaeologists from the Iowa State University Archaeological Laboratory began the excavation. Professor David Gradwohl and research associate Nancy Osborn directed the team, composed of Christy Rickers, Paula Puffer, Kirk Freeman, and Jeff Berland. They had a difficult time working in the confined area under the rooms, where it was hot and dirty and there was little space to maneuver. The archaeologists carefully mapped the soil deposits and tagged and numbered the artifacts area as they dug. The main purpose of the dig was to remove enough fill to provide space to add supports under the floors of these two rooms. As the soil was removed, however, the crew carefully screened every bucketful for artifacts. Gradwohl and Osborn reported that they recovered an extensive number of artifacts, including fragments of porcelain dishes and stoneware containers, a clay smoking pipe, glass and shell buttons, glass bottle fragments, broken glass kerosene lamp chimneys, a scrap of newspaper dated 1901, and a cylindrical dry-cell battery with a patent date of 1893. Also found were animal bones, some of which showed signs of being butchered.

To determine the depth of the foundation for the wooden addition, the team dug a trench outside the house on the east wall near the exterior cellar door. The archaeologists determined that the foundation under the wooden rooms was extremely shallow. Gradwohl reported that it was a "mere three courses of bricks which were well above the frost line." During the excavations, the team also discovered segments of a previous brick foundation running north to south which does not correspond to any of the historical or present walls of the Farm House Museum and cannot be explained at present. In addition, the team unearthed an area covered with paving bricks which corroborated a report in the Board of Trustees minutes from the late 1860s stating that a brick courtyard existed on the north side of the original house.

Osborn also reported that they found evidence of charred floor joists at the east end of the crawl space. Gradwohl said these finds were significant because they revealed evidence of possible previous construction. The charred floor joists, he wrote, "suggest that a portion of the Farm House may once have burned. If this is true, then one might expect evidence of more than one structural renovation at this locus."

While the excavation proceeded, so many additional metal supports were placed under the floors of the main portion of the house
that the basement began to resemble a forest of metal trees. Support
beams were added beneath the wooden rooms as the depth of the dig
allowed. In June the archaeologists ran into asbestos insulation
wrapped around some pipes, so the university's Office of Environ-
mental Health and Safety had to close down the excavation. Gradwohl
estimated that 90 percent of the excavation was complete, resulting in
the many boxes of artifacts now stored in the attic of the house. Fortunately, sufficient floor supports had been added before the area was
closed off and the entire floor support system could be completed by
the end of June.

The celebration of the Farm House Museum's fifteenth year, on
July 4, 1991, was a rousing success. The staff had breathed a sigh of
relief, knowing that the house interior was now successfully braced

University Museum
volunteers Phyllis and
John Thurston and curator
Mary Atherly at the 15th
anniversary celebration of
the opening of the Farm
House Museum, July 4,
1991.

for the large number of expected visitors. The afternoon was reminiscent of that first picnic, held on the Fourth of July in 1858, to celebrate the selection of the site for the college and model farm. Over 500 people attended the 1991 celebration. The Sweet Adelines, the Ametones, and the Tarnished Brass provided musical entertainment while visitors sat on the lawn and ate their meals or participated in games that were located all around the house. Special guest Martin Jischke, then Iowa State University's president, had the honor of cutting the anniversary cake. Visitors wrote greetings to future visitors to the Farm House Museum and placed them in a cardboard time capsule encased in aluminum foil, to be opened in the year 2016. It was later moved to the attic of the house to be stored along with the recovered artifacts.

Even though the fifteenth anniversary celebration went well, the museum staff realized that multiple problems were beginning to surface on the exterior of the house. While the interior was now secure, large cracks had been discovered in the stucco and rotting wood on the pillars of the porches, signs that the Farm House faced another major struggle in the long battle toward restoration.

9 · Exterior Restoration: One Hundred Forty Years Later, a Facelift

*I*n the fall of 1991 volunteers helped the museum staff with a general cleanup day around the Farm House Museum in preparation for winter. While washing exterior windows, curator Mary Atherly noticed a significant number of new cracks in the stucco as well as areas of rotting wood on the west porch columns, so was faced with developing a plan for major exterior repairs and finding the funds to pay for them.

Its status as a National Historic Landmark qualified the Farm House Museum for grants to fund architectural assessments. This type of evaluation was needed to provide accurate information and documentation for the conservation plan, so Atherly began her work by applying for such a grant.

Late in 1991 the museum staff received word that the National Institute for the Conservation of Cultural Property had approved the museum staff's application. With this grant the museum staff was able to hire architect Daniel J. Prosser, a member of the American Institute of Architects, to conduct the assessment, which was scheduled for the following September. Ultimately, Prosser's evidence of serious deterioration on the exterior of the Farm House would begin a nine-year process of more reports, updated evaluations, and revised and expanded plans—all culminating in a costly but necessary renovation to preserve the Farm House.

While awaiting Prosser's arrival, the museum staff kept busy with its schedule of activities and some new developments. During the hot August of 1992, two new student employees scraped and painted the original radiators on the first and second floors of the house. That fall the university administration approved a new position at the museum. For the first time the Farm House Museum's curator would have an assistant. To the delight of Atherly, who was now also serving as the University Museums collections manager, Eleanor

Ostendorf eagerly took over the day-to-day activities of the Farm House. As one of her first projects, Ostendorf did a major wash-down of the west and north porches in preparation for Parents Weekend at the university.

Because of the demands of tours, receptions, and events, it became increasingly difficult for the museum staff to function in the work kitchen that also served as an office and storage area. At times it was difficult to reach the sink because so many artifacts (such as a spinning wheel, dining room chairs, two metal filing cabinets, boxes of glassware and textiles) were stored in the kitchen. To alleviate the congestion, Atherly and University Museums director Lynette Pohlman decided to use the large southwest bedroom on the second floor as office and storage space, but first a massive bed and dresser from that bedroom had to be dismantled and stored in the available closets. With a larger storage area, the small northwest bedroom that had previously been used for storage was emptied of all unnecessary furniture and then reopened to the public.

Daniel Prosser arrived on campus in September 1992 to begin a thorough conservation assessment of the house, inside and out. During his inspection of the basement, Prosser noted that the support jacks and beams added the previous year were already leaning and would require additional supports to straighten them. Paul Rietz, the structural engineer who oversaw the 1991 floor reinforcement project, reviewed Prosser's concerns and ordered several additional supports for the floors, then he assured the curator that the floors were safe for museum visitors. Prosser's concerns for the interior of the house were minor. On his advice new valves and modern thermostats were installed on each radiator in the house, making it possible for the first time to individually control the heat in each room.

Once outside, Prosser documented the damage to the east corner of the exterior south wall where the stucco was deteriorating. He reported that "a combination of clinging vines, shade, and a downspout that discharges directly to the ground at the foundation has encouraged moisture to penetrate the stucco and led the stucco to break loose from the brick masonry behind it." The beautiful ivy vines that lined the exterior south and west walls had to be removed and the bushes cut back. His inspection also showed that the west porch soffit had water damage and portions of the stuccoed columns had cracks. He suggested that if the west porch structure wasn't repaired soon, complete reconstruction might be necessary. Reconstruction eventually did take place, but not until 1999.

In January 1993 the curator sent the university's physical plant

Cellar beneath original kitchen, looking south, 1992.
Photograph by Daniel J. Prosser, Courtesy of Farm House Museum Archives

Southeast front of Farm House, showing ivy vine and expanding crack
in the stucco, 1992.
Photograph by Daniel J. Prosser, Courtesy of Farm House Museum Archives

Northwest porch pier, loose stucco and decay of wood trim and soffit, 1992.
Photograph by Daniel J. Prosser, Courtesy of Farm House Museum Archives

a request for estimates on the repairs recommended by Prosser. Included with the request was Prosser's report, an article on historic stucco, and a reminder that all repairs should take into consideration the house's National Historic Landmark status.

The spring weather of 1993 brought almost constant rain, setting the stage for major flooding in Ames and Des Moines during July. Fortunately, the builders of the Farm House had located it on the highest point on the college farm, but the Scheman Building, which houses the University Museums office and exhibit area, was flooded with eight feet of water. During that summer all University Museums operations were moved into the kitchen and curator's offices at the Farm House Museum. The silver lining to this arrangement was that the extra staff provided the opportunity to open the house on a daily basis.

The hot, humid weather of 1993 caused more cracks in the stucco. During the curator's routine inspection of the damaged stucco on the front of the house, a large four-by-four-foot section of stucco broke away from the house, revealing crumbling soft red bricks and disintegrating mortar. Oddly enough, one visitor to the house said it was very clever of the museum to remove the stucco so visitors could see the original brick!

In October 1993, Iowa State's Department of Facilities Planning and Management prepared a rough estimate of exterior repairs and projected a cost of $40,900 for stucco-work, gutters, downspouts, work on the pillars of the west and south porches, replacement of wood soffits and trim, and painting. The brickwork and tuck-pointing would add another $9,000 to the cost. They suggested that most of the work be done by outside contractors. Because of the high cost estimates, the museum staff requested another estimate for just the stucco replacement. In November 1993, Roger L. Graden from the facilities planning and management department submitted a new estimate stating that at least 50 percent of the stucco would need to be removed in order to analyze the condition of the brickwork underneath. It was already evident that mortar in the area of the exposed brick wall in the southeast corner of the building was severely deteriorated and

Southeast corner of Farm House showing the area where the first stucco detached from bricks, 1993.
Photograph by Mary E. Atherly, Courtesy of Farm House Museum Archives

Graden expected this would be true elsewhere. The brickwork would need to be repaired before new stucco was applied and the rusted downspouts attached to the stucco would need to be removed and replaced. His new estimate for brickwork, stucco-work, and new copper downspouts came to $37,800. Faced with the high costs for exterior repairs, the museum staff requested additional funding from the university. In the meantime, Friends of the University Museums (formerly Friends of the Brunnier and Farm House) donated funds to replace the sidewalk leading to the north porch.

Warren Madden, the university's vice-president for business and finance, visited the Farm House Museum in March 1994 to review the project, resulting in his request that the Farm House project become a priority for year-end building repair funds. This was rejected by the university administration, however, because the museum was not considered academic space. Since University Museums reported to Reid W. Crawford, vice-president for external affairs, Madden wrote to him in July, asking for his assistance. Crawford met with Lynette Pohlman and told her that he would request year-end funds from President Martin Jischke. The museum received a notice from the facilities planning and management department in August that Crawford's request for repairs was backlogged due to insufficient building repair funds.

While concerns for the exterior of the house were ever present, the Farm House Museum staff continued to host events and programs. In December 1994, the Holiday Gift Shoppe opened using space in the old kitchen. Volunteer Kay Beckett managed the shop and made many of the objects that were for sale. It was a financial success. In early 1995, the curator opened an exhibit featuring, for the first time, photographs of past residents of the Farm House. During the spring months, the museum staff gave tours to over 500 people, including school groups, senior citizens, and local social groups. The Alumni Days event on June 8 at the Farm House Museum was a book signing for the recently released *Farm House: College Farm to University Museum* authored by curator Mary Atherly. Two hundred people attended the event.

In 1996, Prosser's report was four years old, so the curator again applied for a grant to have an architectural historian review the exterior of the Farm House Museum and prepare a new plan of action for conservation. In the meantime, Atherly received word that the Farm House Museum had been granted official accreditation by the American Association of Museums, which helped in applying for grants.

During the summer of 1996 the museum staff met with members of the university's facilities planning and management staff, who agreed to make some immediate repairs to the exterior of the house and to replace the leaking hot and cold water lines for the kitchen. Members of Friends of the University Museums volunteered in October to clean, paint, and do yard work to prepare the Farm House Museum for winter. Also in the fall, the museum staff hired a nationally recognized architectural consultant, Martin Weaver, for the conservation assessment project. This was possible because of a generous donation from John and Dorothy McNee of Ames and a grant from Iowa's Resource Enhancement and Protection Act that was channeled through a Historical Resource Development Program managed by the State Historical Society of Iowa.

Weaver arrived in April 1997 and spent a week assessing the exterior and interior of the house. At one point in his inspection, when he tapped the stucco on the west porch columns to determine how secure it was, it came off in sheets, revealing that the porch columns were not solid brick. Weaver found that the "apparently massive and solid columns of the West porch were mere brick shells, 4 ½ inches or half a brick thick with a timber post inside each pier to carry the

Conservator Martin Weaver examines the west porch columns, 1997.
Photograph by Mary E. Atherly, Courtesy of Farm House Museum Archives

roof loads." When Weaver discovered evidence of termite damage in the internal wood post, the curator immediately called on the university's entomologists, who determined that although the insects were long gone, they had caused severe structural damage. Weaver ordered immediate supports for the porch and assisted the university staff in shoring up its roof.

Another of Weaver's immediate concerns was the deteriorating brickwork and mortar on the southwest and southeast corners of the house. He concluded that these two areas urgently needed repair and that to prevent any further problems it was imperative that the brickwork be completed by bricklayers familiar with the nature of antique handmade soft bricks and the type of mortar used in 1912. In accordance with Weaver's recommendations, emergency bids were solicited for the brickwork on the corners of the house.

At the conclusion of his visit, Weaver presented his findings at a fundraising dinner held at the Farm House Museum. He recommended that all the stucco be removed and replaced, explaining that "the stucco, unfortunately, was based on a mixture of Portland Cement and without any lime. It was applied to the brick surfaces,

Exposed deteriorating bricks on the southwest foundation of Farm House, 1997.
Courtesy of Farm House Museum Archives

which were first hacked with a mason's pick to provide a 'key' or mechanical bond." Now these exposed bricks were absorbing moisture, and he feared for damage to the interior walls. Weaver also reported that the basement's brick floors were excessively damp, with visible fungal growth. He recommended repair of the basement windows and installation of a ventilation system to help dry out the entire area. (This was finally completed in the year 2000.)

Weaver's final report, dated April 1997, included recommendations for the interior and exterior of the house. Friends of the University Museums immediately donated $4,000 toward the project.

Southeast corner of Farm House after sheets of stucco delaminated from the bricks, 1997.
Courtesy of Farm House Museum Archives

That summer, Pohlman allocated funds to have an estimate prepared for the projected conservation plan outlined by Weaver and to pay for the emergency brick repairs to the southeast and southwest corners of the house. In July Mike Parsons of Western Waterproofing in Des Moines completed these emergency brickwork repairs.

The facilities planning and management department hired Jim Stecker of Stecker-Harmsen, Inc., of Ames, to provide the basic estimate for other repairs recommended in Weaver's report. The staggering $330,000 estimate included installation of a new shake-shingle roof on the main house, removal of the west porch and its complete reconstruction with a copper roof, removal of all stucco, tuck-pointing all bricks, application of new stucco, and the addition of copper downspouts. The estimate also included installation of a mobility-impaired entry to the front porch.

The University Museums staff began an intensive fundraising campaign in the fall of 1997. In September, former Iowa State University president W. Robert Parks addressed a letter to friends and alumni of the College of Agriculture, urging them to donate toward the Farm House Museum conservation project. Friends of the University Museums took up the fundraising challenge and spent weeks making phone calls to potential donors. By November, the College of Agriculture pledged $50,000 and President Jischke pledged another $50,000 from university funds toward the overall goal. That same month, Warren Madden notified Lynette Pohlman that the Farm House Museum renovation project was now considered a capital project since it was over $250,000 and thus would require the approval of the Iowa Board of Regents. The university planned to include the Farm House Museum project in their requests to the Board of Regents, who would meet in December.

On December 11, 1997, Pohlman and Atherly met with facilities planning and management staff members Scott Sankey and Tim Fogue to outline a timeline for the conservation project. As architect, Fogue would prepare plans for the bids and Sankey would prepare a budget and schedule. Atherly was designated the project manager for the museums and she also agreed to contact Judy McClure at the State Historical Society of Iowa to communicate Sankey's concerns regarding the nature of the historic site. Martin Weaver continued to be the architectural consultant. It was expected that the entire project, with contingency funds, would top $350,000. Bid documents were completed in March 1998 and forwarded to Martin Weaver for his comments. Bids from contractors were expected on July 21, 1998.

While fundraising for the exterior work continued, the museum staff provided regular maintenance on the interior of the house. New curtains were added to the library and window shades to the upstairs bedroom windows. They donned protective plastic shower caps and painted the ceilings in the kitchen and education rooms. Family events continued to bring in a large number of visitors. The Victorian Holidays events brought in 1,636 visitors during December 1997. A family Farm Day held in May 1998 drew a crowd of 500 people, all clamoring to pet the small animals exhibited by students from Iowa State's College of Veterinary Medicine.

The Farm House Museum closed on June 9, 1998, in anticipation of the start of the conservation project. The staff removed from the walls everything that was not permanently affixed. All the furniture was covered with white sheets, the rugs were rolled and covered, the curtains and shades were removed. The inside of the house took on a ghostly white appearance.

The morning of July 21, 1998, curator Atherly hurried across campus to the physical plant building to be present when bids on the conservation project were opened. Unfortunately, there were no bids! Scott Sankey suggested the problems could be that the vigorous construction season was already under way and that the house was a National Historic Landmark with specific federal standards for conservation. Whatever the reasons, Sankey suggested waiting until January to send out another request for bids. Reluctantly, the University Museums staff agreed.

Parlor of Farm House decorated for Victorian Holidays, December 1997.
Courtesy of Farm House Museum Archives

The Farm House Museum reopened in August when the students returned for fall semester. During the summer the staff had done a thorough cleaning of the house. Fundraising continued with special events at the Farm House Museum. The good news was that donations for the conservation project now totaled $265,000. Delaying the construction project gave the curator time to apply for a State Historical Society of Iowa Historic Site Preservation Grant. In the application due on September 14, 1998, the curator requested $92,000, with a cash match of $228,000 from the University Museums.

The second public hearing on bids for the conservation project took place on February 1, 1999. This time two bids were received. The university awarded the contract to the lower of the two bidders, Welker Construction of Marshalltown, Iowa. With a base bid of $243,200 and an alternate bid on the west porch of $63,300, which included a copper roof, Welker's proposed construction starting date was April 1, 1999.

More good news came in February. The State Historical Society of Iowa awarded a grant for the exterior conservation of the Farm House Museum in the amount of $75,000, stipulating that if more funds became available later the grant could go as high as $92,000. One provision of the grant was for an archaeological investigation of areas around the house that would be disturbed by construction, in particular the east window well. Professor Joseph Tiffany of the university's anthropology department agreed to manage the archaeological dig, which needed to be completed prior to any on-site digging.

Pohlman and Atherly met with facilities planning and management staff in early March 1999 to go over several issues. They agreed to save the west porch foundation, to reuse all the porch and window screens if possible, to use Portland Cement for the stucco (which was approved by the U.S. Parks Service), and to install a copper roof on the west porch. The Department of Facilities Planning and Management also agreed not to bill their usual administrative fees, which amounted to a savings of $14,000.

Sherman Welker, head contractor at Welker Construction, Troy Lux, Welker's project superintendent, and representatives of Kennedy Plaster Company met with university and museum staff on March 31, for a preconstruction review. Bob Catus was the construction project manager for the university and contact for the museums. Concerns about schedule, lead time, site use, and coordination were discussed. Also at issue was the process for the application of new stucco. Welker had subcontracted it to Kennedy Plaster Company, which stated that it could not guarantee the stucco-work unless they placed metal lath over the bricks before applying it. They also suggested use of corner anchors. It was finally agreed that Kennedy could use the metal lath, even though it had not been used in the original stucco application.

In early April Iowa State's archaeological team began excavation of the east window wells. Physical plant personnel carefully removed the remaining shrubs around the windows to allow the clear five-foot area next to the wells the archaeological team wanted for their work. Tina N. Nepstad-Thornberry, under the direction of Professor Tiffany, directed the dig. She stated in her final report that "the results of the Phase 1 testing of the areas adjacent to the two window wells were negative. No further work is warranted." Bricks, plaster, flat glass, wire nails, and a single fragment of whiteware decorated with a blue spongeware pattern were recovered from the site, none of significant value. These cataloged artifacts are stored in the attic of the Farm House Museum along with the artifacts from previous digs.

Once again the museum staff removed objects from the interior walls, rolled up rugs, and covered furniture with sheets in anticipation of the construction. The museum closed on March 31, 1999, hoping to reopen in early fall at the completion of the conservation efforts.

Before beginning any work on the site, Welker spent two days taking photographs to document the existing details of the house. The project began on the west porch area. All the screens were saved and stored, as were the balusters on the porch roof, to be used as templates for new ones. The rest of the porch structure was demolished except for the floor and foundation. Welker's crew nailed large sheets of plywood across the French doors to protect the glass and over the red tile porch floor to protect the surface. Removing the stucco was tedious work. Several pieces of it were saved so that the stucco contractor could match the consistency. While tearing off the stucco on the west wall of the house in the porch area, the workers discovered an original bricked-up doorway where students in the 1870s had entered the Farm House for their field assignments.

As the crew worked around the house removing stucco, they nailed more plywood sheets over windows for protection. Inside, the house became dark, hot, and humid. Outside, the ground was wet from rain and deep tire tracks appeared where work trucks and equipment moved on and off the site. The lawn soon vanished.

On April 28, 1999, Atherly wrote, "I saw the front of the Farm House for the first time in its original redbrick face. I really love it.

View of west side of Farm House following demolition of screened porch, 1999.
Photograph by Mary E. Atherly, Courtesy of Farm House Museum Archives

Manual removal of stucco begins on south side of Farm House, 1999.
Photograph by Mary E. Atherly, Courtesy of Farm House Museum Archives

South front of Farm House showing exposed original 1860s bricks,
1999.
Photograph by Mary E. Atherly, Courtesy of Farm House Museum Archives

North side of Farm House following removal of stucco and the north
chimney, 1999.
Photograph by Mary E. Atherly, Courtesy of Farm House Museum Archives

Too bad we can't leave the stucco off and return it to its former self."
Many other people walking past the project also expressed this opinion. Without the stucco, the house was completely different in appearance and truly looked like a nineteenth-century farmhouse. Unfortunately, the old brick was deemed too soft to be exposed to the
weather, so plans to restucco the exterior continued.

Almost daily, Atherly documented the work by taking colored
slides and digital photos. These images were put on the Web site of
the University Museums so that the public could follow the renovation progress.

By May 5, all the old stucco was gone from the chimneys and
house. There were two large holes in the north chimney where bricks
were missing, and previous repairs to this chimney were evident. In
all, three of the five chimneys were structurally unstable after the
stucco was removed and required demolition and reconstruction,
adding $6,500 to the cost of the project. It seemed that every day
brought a new problem to light. Each addition to the project meant
more expenses. On behalf of the museums, the university requested
and received approval from the Board of Regents for a revised project budget that increased the initial project by $27,000. On the other
hand, some things remained in the dark. Evidence of a bricked-up
stovepipe hole, which Atherly had hoped would solve the mystery of
where the early Farm House residents cooked, never did appear.

Work continued on the west porch with the removal of the concrete base. Before pouring a new one, the crew laid steel rods inside
the frames. Once the base was poured they built two substantial
square-cornered support columns, each with a concrete block on all
four sides and a small open area in the middle.

On the south side of the house, workers removed the ceiling
from the south front porch so they could rebuild the roof. The construction crew nailed boards in an X pattern across the sides and
front of the porch to keep people off. Unfortunately, repairs to this
porch also required more extensive reconstruction than was originally anticipated. Because the porch footings did not extend to the
point noted on the original drawings, the support structure for the
porch roof was found to be inadequate and had to be dismantled. The
porch columns, bases, and capitals were repaired where possible.
Where repair was not possible, woodwork samples were taken to a
millwork shop so that dimensions could be matched for new pieces.
The workers rebuilt the entire south porch from the foundation up,
laying a solid brick foundation before adding a new floor and rein-

The west porch during reconstruction, 1999.
Photograph by Mary E. Atherly, Courtesy of Farm House Museum Archives

stalling the original columns. To give access to the proposed west
sidewalk, they removed the middle portion of the west side rails of
the porch. Later, flower boxes were added to the top of the remaining rails. A new copper roof with gutter and downspouts completed
the porch.

Again, new discoveries brought increased expenses and delayed
the completion date. There was a large break in the lower wall and
foundation on the northwest corner of the house, leaving the interior
of the basement visible from the outside. Atherly and Ostendorf
stuffed plastic bags and pieces of Styrofoam into the holes to prevent
rain and critters from getting in. Also, bricks were missing from the
outer layers of a small area in this same corner. The brickwork on the
wall was repaired and missing bricks were replaced using Chicago
bricks similar to the original 1860 ones and eventually the foundation
repairs were complete.

Kira Kaufmann, archaeologist for the State Historical Society of
Iowa, visited the Farm House Museum on July 19, 1999. During her

Front of Farm House after
removal of south porch,
1999.
*Photograph by Mary E.
Atherly, Courtesy of Farm
House Museum Archives*

visit, she learned that the contractor proposed digging a large hole
adjacent to the northwest foundation in order to repair a crack. Kaufmann said an archaeological investigation of the area was necessary
before this hole could be dug, so Professor Joseph Tiffany agreed to
direct this new excavation. The area under investigation was where a
garage had been attached to the house in the 1920s but was later removed. After twelve auger tests, the only find was the 1920s concrete
garage foundation. Tiffany wrote, "Heavy disturbance of the area
north of the Farm House Museum was observed," and that "no archaeological features or structures would be directly impacted by
trench work along the north foundation." Repair work there was com-

Workers reconstruct the front south porch reusing original columns, 1999. *Photograph by Mary E. Atherly, Courtesy of Farm House Museum Archives*

pleted in November after the representatives of the State Historical Society were satisfied that digging in the area would not disturb an archaeologically significant area.

In August, representatives from the State Historical Society of Iowa met with the construction team to discuss a landscape plan for the house and the possible location of a mobility-impaired sidewalk on the south side of the house. The plans called for the walk to extend from an adjacent west campus sidewalk to the west side of the south porch. Both Pohlman and Atherly wanted the house to be more visible to the campus and requested no new plantings be placed along the west side of the yard. They also requested that grass be planted up to the foundation of the house as it had been in 1912 when the house was first stuccoed. This minimal landscape plan was approved.

After the porches were rebuilt, roofers began working on the shake-shingle roof which covered the main area of the house. They installed copper roofs—actually small squares of copper welded together—on the south, north, and west porches. Installation required expert and delicate work by the construction crew. Copper was also used in the downspouts and gutters, which were attached after the final coating of stucco. It was originally thought the copper would eventually acquire the typical green patina, but an air-quality test showed Ames air to lack the acid that causes copper to change color. As a consequence, the copper roofs and downspouts have remained a dull brown to this day.

In one of the weekly construction meetings, it had been decided to use a conventional cement-and-lime-based mixture for the new stucco instead of the previously proposed synthetic-based stucco mixture, a change that eventually saved over $15,000. In June, Welker made a mock-up panel of the exterior stucco using the cement-and-

New shake-shingle roof being installed on north side of house, 1999.
Photograph by Mary E. Atherly, Courtesy of Farm House Museum Archives

lime mixture in several different consistencies. Atherly contacted Wesley Shank, the architectural historian who had worked on the 1970 restoration of the Farm House, to ask his opinion about the color to be used. Before the stuccowork could proceed, the subcontractors at Kennedy Plaster Company applied a metal lath over the bricks so the stucco of fiber-reinforced Portland Cement would adhere.

Everyone knew that the stucco had to be reapplied, but it was difficult for many to see the original red bricks disappear again, even for their own protection. By the end of August, Kennedy Plaster Company had completed the application of stucco and the painters were waiting for a decision on whether or not to coat the surface. In early September, Bob Catus asked for clarification on the coating to be used on the stucco. Catus had some samples of a Prosoco clear coating and tested it on some areas of the stucco. After a phone call to Martin Weaver, who recommended using a pigmented coating called KEIM, Catus ordered a sample, which took ten days to arrive on site. Weaver recommended KEIM because it could be applied immediately instead of the normal one-year wait to cure the stucco, and because it had a fifteen-year warranty. Manufactured in Europe, with only one

Replication of original decorative design in stucco above windows, 1999.

Photograph by Mary E. Atherly, Courtesy of Farm House Museum Archives

supplier in the United States, KEIM had a mineral base and was designed to bond with the substrate and become part of the stucco. It was also more expensive than Prosoco. After reviewing the test sample areas, however, the construction team selected KEIM 5004, a gray from the KEIM Historical Collection. Bob Catus immediately placed an order.

The painters working on the wood trim were anxious to get the coating started on the stucco. The curator checked on the work progress daily and tried to keep a positive attitude while the painters kept asking when the KEIM coating was going to arrive. It took two weeks from the September 20 order date for the coating to arrive on site. One week later, the stucco coating was completed.

Once that was complete, some finishing touches were added to the house. New copper downspouts directed rainwater away from the house and basement area. All the screens from the house were re-hung, with the exception of the southeast window screen, which has never been found. Workers also repaired the window frame on the second-floor landing after removing rotten wood and patching the area.

On Sunday, September 19, 1999, Mary Atherly, Sherman Welker, and Troy Lux gave an overview of the exterior restoration of the Farm House Museum to an enthusiastic audience at the Brunnier Art Museum. It was billed as a "presentation in pictures and words of the challenges and surprises encountered during the six-month project." Atherly was also able to tell the audience the good news that the State Historical Society of Iowa had increased their grant from $75,000 to $92,000.

A month later, Pohlman, Atherly, Catus, and Sankey met to review the budget and to go over the final details of the project. Because of some additional financial donations, several items could be added to the final list, including a metal door on the east basement entrance, copper chimney caps on all five chimneys, two new lights for the west porch, painting of all the windows on the outside, some landscaping, an underground sump pump line extension, and a new redbrick walk on the south side of the house. Both the west and south sidewalks needed to be in place before the house could be opened to the public.

After Welker removed his work trailer and equipment from the yard, Iowa State's physical plant staff began laying sod on the west side of the Farm House Museum. Once the sidewalks were installed, the grounds crew finished with the front lawn. It was late November, but the weather remained warm so the grass could be watered. The

South side of Farm House, 2007.
Photograph by Bob Elbert, Courtesy Iowa State University

West side of Farm House showing new sidewalk and porch entrance, 2007.
Photograph by Bob Elbert, Courtesy of Iowa State University

A view of the north side of Farm House, 2007.
Photograph by Bob Elbert, Courtesy of Iowa State University

museum staff reopened the Farm House Museum to the public on Sunday, November 28, 1999, at the start of the winter season's Victorian Holidays.

As with any construction project, small problems with the original work soon needed attention. In the spring of 2000, minor cracks in the stucco were repaired and additional work was completed on the flashing on the north side of the house. Atherly, Catus, Pohlman, and Sankey met in April 2000 to review the final project budget. Construction costs totaled $356,685. The source of funds included $50,000 from the general university funds, $92,000 from the Iowa Historic Site Preservation Grant, $50,000 from the College of Agriculture, and the balance from private donations.

Before the museum signed off on the project, a final checklist was made. Atherly felt great satisfaction in being able to see the project through to completion before she retired as curator at the end of the year. Eleanor Ostendorf became acting curator and served until her retirement in the summer of 2007.

East side of Farm House with copper downspouts and metal basement entry door, 2007.
Photograph by Bob Elbert, Courtesy of Iowa State University

Research on the house and its residents continues. New discoveries add to the historical integrity of the Farm House Museum. In a forgotten pile of lumber in the basement of the house, two sections of a gate were discovered that correspond to a photo taken in the 1920s. When Helen Curtiss, who was born in the house in 1901, graduated from college, she had designed a gate for the arbor, located adjacent to the well on the north side of the house. It featured two facing birds on either side of the gate. The Iowa State graduating class of 2002 commissioned the reconstruction of the arbor and the gate as a class project (U2002.34). It is fabricated of Osage orange and Eastern red cedar wood. Today, a grape vine once again covers the arbor.

One issue that always puzzled Lynette Pohlman (who wrote her graduate thesis on the 1970s interior renovation of the Farm House) was the location of the fireplace in Charles Curtiss's first-floor library. Documents showed it had been built around 1912 but removed in a 1940s renovation. In June 2006, Pohlman hired Randy Fiscus of Iowa State's facilities planning and management department to help remove portions of the wall in the library where she believed the fire-

Reconstructed garden gate and arbor, northeast area of yard, 2006.
Courtesy of Farm House Museum Archives

place was located. She also called architect Wesley Shank, who was on the original Farm House committee, for his expert assistance. Fiscus first removed small sections of wallpaper along the east wall, then a section of plaster and bricks that exposed evidence of a firebox. Pohlman was delighted to discover the fireplace location and began a campaign to raise funds for its reconstruction. The fireplace reconstruction project took less than a year to complete with the assistance of generous donations from friends of the museum.

On March 22, 2007, Iowa State University began its year-long celebration of the 150th anniversary of its establishment with an all-day open house at the Farm House Museum, the Brunnier Art Museum, and the new Christian Petersen Museum at Morrill Hall. How would the original founders of the college react if they could see the growth of the college from the small Farm House and one college building to today's campus? One thing is certain: they would be profoundly touched by the efforts of those who accomplished so much with so few resources.

Reconstructed fireplace in the southeast library on the first floor, 2007.
Photograph by Bob Elbert, Courtesy of Iowa State University

Many questions still remain about the Farm House. What exactly is the significance of the separate foundation wall discovered under the east kitchen during the 1991 excavation? What happened to cause the damage to the charred floor beams uncovered by the archaeologists? Was there ever a stovepipe hole in the original northwest kitchen wing? If not, how did residents cook and heat in this part of the house before the 1890s? We may never know all the names of the people who lived in the house throughout the years, but we hope that readers of this second edition will be able to help us identify more of those who made the Farm House their home.

The Farm House is no longer a lonely house on the wild prairie. Today a modern university campus surrounds it. As a museum and National Historic Landmark, it continues to be a lasting symbol of the humble beginnings of Iowa State University. The Farm House has benefited from the nation's interest in sprucing up its National Historic Landmark sites for the 1976 bicentennial celebration and from the generosity of the many alumni and visitors who provided most of the funding to renovate the exterior of the house in the 1990s.

A multitude of programs, events, and tours at the Farm House Museum continue to inform and entertain thousands of visitors each year. The Farm House remains significant to Iowa State University and the nation not because of its unique architectural appearance but because of the people who lived there. Each individual, including college presidents, farm laborers, students, farm superintendents, and deans of agriculture, contributed in their own special way to the success of Iowa's agricultural land-grant college.

Appendix A
Brief Architectural History of the Farm House

Wesley Shank

*T*he gray stuccoed house we see today is essentially the house as it stood in 1914, when the dean of agriculture of Iowa State College and his family lived in it. As originally completed, and until the late 19th century, the house looked very different. The walls were redbrick, an ornate verandah stretched across the front of the house, and no screened porch stood at the side. Then the managers and superintendents of the college farm lived there with their families and used part of the house as an office.

The Nineteenth Century

The main block of the house was a simple two-story rectangle facing south. A lower single-story wing with an attic extending back from the western edge of the rear of the house formed the kitchen wing. (See illustrations of the floor plans in Chapter 1.) At the formal entrance, the front-door transom and sidelights lighted the central hallway. The present large first-floor room taking up the whole west side of the house originally may have been two rooms. We know that the farm manager's or superintendent's office was here originally, and an old photograph shows that it had its own outside door at the west side of the house. An interesting decorative feature of the interior design is the way the top edges of many of the door frames are shaped like a pediment (sloping roof).

At the back of the house two wood-frame structures were connected at the kitchen, forming a courtyard enclosed on three sides. The first structure, which connected to the north end of the kitchen wing, served as a washroom, milk room, and woodshed. The second structure was a wood house and workshop, but it also served as a place "for the hands to spend their leisure hours." Close by were two small brick structures: a double privy, for the house had no indoor

217

plumbing, and a building that was a smokehouse and ash house. Paved walks led to these buildings. The cellar of the house itself, reached by the stairway in the kitchen wing, was used for storage of potatoes and vegetables.

Some of the materials and labor for the house and the barn were donated by people who lived in this part of the county, and some materials were taken from the site. The foundation of the house is rubble limestone, rough stone taken from a donated quarry about a mile and a half west of the house. Lime for mortar and plaster was available in the locality. The bricks for the walls were made on the farm using the clay from the site, and the timber in the building came from the farm as well. In the mid-19th century people working by hand with the broadax would often hew logs into large square timbers on the site. The logs to be cut into joists and boards, however, were hauled to a sawmill, where they were cut by a water- or steam-powered circular saw. In the cellar and the attic we can see the hewn timber beams of the floor and roof framing, with the marks of the broadax still on their surfaces. The surfaces of the joists show the marks of a circular saw. The beams are notched, and the joists which they support rest in the notches. It is interesting that some of the main dimensions of the house are based on a 16-foot module, or sometimes half of that module, a practice common in traditional construction before the Industrial Revolution. The side of the main block of the house is 32 feet; the ends and side of the kitchen wing are 16 feet and 24 feet; and the washroom, milk room, and woodshed structure in back of the kitchen is 24 feet square.

The Farm House in the 19th century lacked many conveniences that we take for granted. Wood-burning stoves heated the house and the one in the kitchen was also the cookstove. By the time the Farm House was built, people preferred to heat their houses with cast-iron or lightweight sheet-metal stoves rather than fireplaces because the stoves used less fuel. In addition, the small sheet-metal stoves, along with the stovepipes that fed into the brick chimneys, were easy to take apart and store in the summer. A circular metal cover, which was often decorated, closed the pipe openings in the wall of the chimney. Natural breezes through open windows and doors helped cool the house in summer, and the natural light the windows admitted was important in all seasons. Oil lamps and candles were used at night. Water had to be carried in from a well, and the only way to get hot water was to heat it on the kitchen stove. Lacking indoor plumbing, people had to walk outside to the privy, or use chamber pots.

The engraving from A. T. Andreas' 1875 *Illustrated Historical At-*

las of the State of Iowa gives us an idea of the site and the surroundings of the house. The picture shows the back part of the house, the large cattle and horse barns northeast of it, and the nearby fenced enclosures. (See illustration on page 53.) We know that a sheep barn and windmill stood not far away, but they are not shown. The trees clustered near the house are probably the ones planted, along with a lawn and some shrubbery, in 1865. A map of the college in H. S. Day's *Iowa State University Campus and Its Buildings, 1859-1979,* shows central campus of 1875 as a large area devoid of buildings with a road circling it. The Farm House and the barns appear at the northeast end of this area. At the south was the college president's house and at the west were the rest of the college buildings.

Of the people associated with the original design and construction of the Farm House whose names are known, Milens Burt of Muscatine was very important. He appears to have been its designer and was described as "architect and builder, a prudent, judicious, and excellent mechanic." Burt's plan of the house and barn was submitted to the legislature along with the first annual report of the secretary of the college for 1858 and 1859. No copy of the plan is known to have survived, so we cannot say for sure that the design is his. Those who worked on the house or supplied materials for it included W. J. Graham, who did plastering; John Freeman, who did plastering and brickwork; R. M. Kellogg, who supplied "sundries" and worked on the house; Benjamin & Cole, who supplied paints and oils; T. Walkup, who supplied lumber, doors, and blinds (the 19th-century term for shutters); O. H. White, who supplied lightning rods; and E. C. Rock, who supplied hardware and a stove.

The funds for the house were appropriated by the state legislature. The total dollar cost of the completed house as it stood in 1865 can be given as $3,275.42, the sum of expenses listed by the Board of Trustees for 1864 and 1865. Of course, the value of the house was greater, for much of the material and labor had been donated.

The parts of the Farm House were built in sequence. The kitchen wing was begun first, in 1860, and was finished by February 1861. Construction on the main block of the house was started in 1861 and was substantially complete in the spring of 1864. The front verandah was built in 1865, along with the outbuildings. The house was described in 1865 as finished, except for painting and inside work.

A number of changes were made in the house during the 19th century. In 1871 the superintendent's office was moved out of the west side of the first floor of the house, and the two east rooms on the first floor were made into a secretary's office and a reporting room. The former superintendent's office was converted to a parlor, and the kitchen was enlarged. In the following year, water and illuminating gas were piped into the house, using cheap pipe available from Chicago after the Great Fire of 1871. In the mid-1870s, the wood house and workshop structure was repaired and plastered to make a dining room and office for the farm laborers. In 1886, a two-room wood-frame addition was made to the back of the house, and the whole house was remodeled to make it into a two-family dwelling. This indicates the activities formerly conducted in the secretary's office and the reporting room may have been moved elsewhere.

The Civil War broke out in 1861, the year after construction on the Farm House began, and ended in 1865, the same year that the house was completed. The railroad network that had entered the state from the east in the mid-1850s passed through the college farm in 1864, the same year the town of Ames, named for the railroad promoter Oakes Ames, was laid out. In that same year, Iowa became the first state to accept the terms of the Morrill Act which Congress had passed in 1862. This legislation marked the beginning of the research and educational base for modern agriculture. But the Farm House itself represents the preindustrial age that was coming to a close. Its stone was quarried by hand labor, its bricks were made on the site by hand, and its large timbers were hand hewn. Mortar, nails, and building hardware were made by artisans in small shops. Building materials were still hauled by horses and mules and oxen; and laborers and animal power, not machinery, dug cellars and toted building materials.

The two architectural styles for houses in use at the time the Farm House was built were the Gothic Revival style, associated with the warmth and homelike qualities of a cottage, and the Italian Villa style, intended to suggest a country villa. In both styles the floor plan and roof arrangement were often complex and asymmetrical. However, in the previously used Greek Revival style, often appearing with Greek columns and other Greek architectural details, floor plans were symmetrical, roofs simple, and the general appearance massive. Such simple plans and roof forms were in use in later times, just as we see at the Farm House, although in some other respects the design might follow a current architecture style. This conservative continuation of earlier architectural practices is a hallmark of vernacular architecture, the traditional way of building that changes slowly and retains earlier practices. The floor plan of the Farm House is vernacular, just as the construction methods of the house are of the preindustrial era. The origin of its plan predates the Greek Revival style of the early 19th century and lies in the English Georgian architecture brought to the British North American colonies in the 1700s.

The designer of the Farm House, whether Milens Burt or not, consciously chose some of the popular decorative forms of the Italian Villa style: the shallow arch of the brickwork spanning the door and window openings, the pattern of large window panes in the first-floor main rooms, and the ornate verandah (which may, if an afterthought, have been someone else's choice). But the style was used superficially, because basically the architect followed the vernacular to which he was more accustomed.

The Farm House, as it was originally described, was designed to be a farmer's house, with an office from which its principal resident, the farm manager or superintendent, would operate the model farm. The house itself was also thought of as a "model building." The designer, doubtless a practical person, wanted the house to look like what it was, a farmer's house, and the architect would also have followed traditional ideas about what a respectable farm house ought to be. We can see in the orderly design of the building that the architect was conscious of the significance of the house as part of a state institution. That the building was also the office of the farm manager or superintendent was concealed—to enter it directly from the outside, people had to use a side door.

The significance of the original Farm House is principally historical. It is the oldest surviving building on the Iowa State University campus, and it was the home of the several managers and superintendents of the college farm. For a few intervals the house was occupied by presidents of the college and their families. Of these men, Seaman A. Knapp and James F. Wilson were important national figures. The State Agricultural College and Model Farm was the beginning of the present university, which played a key role in bringing about scientific agriculture in the Midwest and has in our time grown to international influence and stature. The basic structure of the original brick house survives in the present building as a testimony to methods of construction in the Midwest before the impact of the Industrial Revolution, and the design of the original house is an example of the work of Iowa builders and probably of a builder-architect of this era.

The Twentieth Century

In 1914 the house looked essentially the way we see it now. A single-car garage at the rear, which dated from the 1920s, has been removed. Knoll Road passed near the house on the east in 1914, as it does now, but the limestone Neoclassical-style Dairy Industry Building on the other side of the road was not built until the late 1920s, and the seven-story limestone classroom building south of the house was not built until the early 1970s. To the west lay central campus, with its open lawns and picturesque groves of mature trees. The large limestone Neoclassical-style buildings there, Beardshear, Marston, and Curtiss halls, were in place in 1914.

The changes that created the present building date from 1897 to 1914. A central heating system was installed by James Wilson, who, when he left to become U.S. secretary of agriculture in the late 1890s, asked to be reimbursed for what it had cost him. During the late 19th century the wooden buildings at the north of the house were torn down, as was the privy. Bathroom facilities and electric lighting were installed. (In 1972 the room at the front of the second-floor hallway was a bathroom, and one of the rooms in the attic of the kitchen wing was also a bathroom.) In 1907 the house was connected to the new central heating plant that had been built for the campus. From about 1910 to 1914, the rest of the work was done. The soft brick walls, which had required constant repainting to protect their crumbling surfaces, were given the hard gray stuccoing that we now see. On the west side of the house, the present large screened porch was built and the first-floor west windows connecting to it were converted to French doors. One undated architectural drawing for the screened porch survives. The drawing bears the name of the Des Moines architectural firm of Proudfoot and Bird, who were at the time the architects for all buildings at the three state institutions of higher learning. It is not known if the firm was responsible for the design of the other changes in the house made during this time. In 1913 funds were appropriated for an asbestos shingle roof. These diamond-shaped light gray shingles remained on the building until it was roofed with wood shingles in 1972. The oak flooring seems to date from after 1914. In 1926 a single-car garage, constructed of hollow clay tile and stuccoed to match the rest of the house, was added to the north wall of the original kitchen wing and in 1948 the kitchen, then occupying the eastern room of the two-room frame addition along the north of the main block of the house, was remodeled.

The Farm House was then the residence of Charles F. Curtiss, the dean of agriculture, and the changes made to it during the early 1900s reflect this fact. Curtiss obtained the funds for the work from the legislature in a number of requests. From 1910 to 1912, $1,541 was spent on repairing the house, and in 1913, $495 was appropriated for the asbestos roofing.

Between 1972 and 1975 work on the house was done to restore it to the appearance it would have had in about 1914, when Dean Curtiss lived in it, and to convert it to a museum. The present wood shingle roof was installed and extensive gutter and chimney repairs were made. The garage was removed. Inside, sagging floors and ceilings were made level and reinforced, and the heating, plumbing, and electrical systems were renovated. The bathroom at the front of the second-floor hallway was removed, which enlarged the hallway. Of the two second-floor rooms in the original kitchen wing, the south one had been remodeled into a bathroom. This was restored to the appearance it might have had, replacing the modern fixtures with appropriate old ones. These have since been removed.

The period when the Farm House took its present form—from 1897 to 1914—included the golden age of agriculture. The efforts of the land-grant agriculture colleges were bearing fruit as the United States began to face a new problem, crop surpluses. World War I, which broke out in Europe in 1914, provided a market for surplus crops and temporarily solved the problem. Scientific farming and the use of farm machinery, powered first by steam and then by the internal combustion engine, had played their part in revolutionizing American agriculture.

Three important late 19th-century architectural styles were present among buildings constructed on the Iowa State campus from 1895 to 1915. Old Botany (originally Agriculture Hall) was an example of the Queen Anne style, Alumni Hall represented the Georgian Revival, and Marston, Beardshear, and Curtiss halls follow the Neoclassic style.

Dean Curtiss functioned in some respects as the designer for the 20th-century changes in the house. His intention seems clear: to make the house into an up-to-date residence appropriate for a college dean. The exterior of the house, largely because of the simplicity of its overall shape, the symmetry of its arrangement of doors and windows, and the classical orders and balustrades of its new porches follows the Classic Revival style more closely than any of the other architectural styles of the time of its modernization.

The house as it stands today has an aesthetic appropriateness that it had previously lacked. Its formality and style are appropriate to its use as the residence of a college dean. The symmetrical massiveness of the main block is in character with the Roman Tuscan columns of the entrance porch and the classic balustrade at the roof of the screened side porch.

In addition to its 19th-century significance, the house is significant in the 20th century because it preserves much of the 19th-century house and the adaptations that were made to it during the first 50 years of its existence to change it from the residence and office of the 19th-century farm manager or superintendent of the State Agricultural College and Model Farm to a modern residence for the dean of agriculture of Iowa State College.

The Twenty-First Century: The First Decade

A significant shortcoming in the efforts during the early 1970s to restore the house to its 1914 appearance was the fact that the fireplace in the library was still missing. Its presence was historically well documented. It had been removed in 1948, the wall where it was had been bricked in flush with the chimney wall above, and matching oak flooring had replaced the hearth. In the cellar below, almost the entire ash pit remained. It would be impossible to restore the fireplace, however, because nobody knew what it looked like. An educated guess might have been made and a reconstructed fireplace built based on that. At the time this was thought unwise, because it seemed likely that a photograph or a detailed description might turn up as a result of the rekindled interest in the building's history.

Thirty-some years later, the hoped-for information still had not appeared. University Museums director Lynette Pohlman sought the advice of several people, including me, on what might be done about the fireplace. The educated-guess possibilities were explored, even to the extent of consulting a respected architectural restoration firm and obtaining drawings and a cost estimate. Not quite comfortable with this alternative, I realized that clues provided by the house itself should be investigated first. Remembering that Margaret Keyes, in directing the restoration work on Old Capitol in the early 1970s, had discovered forgotten fireplaces walled-over in earlier times, I thought that portions of the original library fireplace might lie behind the bricks that closed it in.

In July 2006, the investigation began. Removal of the infill bricks revealed the smoke-blackened bricks of the back of Dean Curtiss's fireplace, portions of its sides, and the lower part of the chimney throat. Removal of the patch in the oak flooring at the base of the chimney showed where the hearth had been. Inspection of the brick ash pit in the cellar revealed that its upper courses had been removed along with the projecting chimneybreast and hearth above it.

Armed with these clues and with information about historic fireplaces, I was able to prepare a reconstruction diagram of a working fireplace that could have been built and connected to the existing chimney. I could determine how far the chimneybreast projected into the room and how high it was. In effect, we now knew with reasonable assurance the probable outlines of the fireplace and the hearth. An educated-guess reconstruction would now be one step closer to the truth, but still only a guess. At this point, I consulted Jan Jennings, historian of interior design at Cornell University, who had taught in the College of Design at Iowa State several years ago. Since the Farm House Museum is a National Historic Landmark, restoration work needed to follow U.S. Department of Interior standards. Based on these Jennings suggested we should use wall surfaces like those in the rest of the room to create a place-marker fireplace that was the probable size and shape of the fireplace and its hearth. In essence, this is what we did, but with a significant innovation. The blackened bricks of the original fireplace opening were incorporated, so that parts of the place-marker are the portions of the original fireplace that have survived. They make clear what is historically authentic and what is intended only to be helpful suggestion. John Byerly, architect, and Randy Fiscus, carpenter, both at Iowa State's Department of Faculties Planning and Management, were involved in the investigation and in the design and construction of the place-marker fireplace.

Appendix B
Residents of the Farm House, Chronological Listing

Residents	Dates
Fitchpatrick family: William H. Fitchpatrick, tenant farmer; wife, Sarah Hagy Fitchpatrick; children, Joseph, William, John, Mary, Martha, Sarah, Nancy, Liza *Note:* William joined the army in the summer of 1861 and Joseph joined in 1863.	March, 1861–March 1863
Sarah Emery, schoolteacher	1862
Graves family: Andrew Jackson Graves, farm manager; wife, Mary M. Meredity Graves; son, Edward Graves, born at the Farm House, July 27, 1864	March 1, 1864–April 10, 1868
Moses W. Robinson, farm superintendent (Did not bring his family)	March 1, 1864–Nov. or Dec. 1866
Hugh M. Thomson, farm superintendent (Did not bring family)	January 24, 1867–September 30, 1869
Gilmore family: James Gilmore, farm manager; wife, Eliza; and children, John, George, Jamie, and Robert	April 11, 1868–late summer 1870
Welch family: Adonijah Welch, president-elect; wife, Mary B. Dudley Welch; children, Harry, William, Genevieve, and Winifred Dudley *Note:* The family moved back to the Farm House in the spring while they were waiting for their home to be completed.	September–November 1868 and spring 1869
A. E. Foote, professor	1868–1870
Norton Townshend, professor	1868–1869
Peter Christensen, farm laborer	1869–1870

Andrew Christensen, farm laborer	1869–1870
Augusta Mathews, music instructor	1869–1870
John Radford, carpenter	1870
Robert McCarey, carpenter	1870
Mary Lewis, housekeeper	1870
Lizzie Williams, housekeeper	1870
Stark family: Nicholas Stark, carpenter; wife, M.(?); children, Charles and Nicholas	1870
Roberts family: Isaac Phillips Roberts, superintendent; wife, Margaret Jane Marr Roberts; two children	August 1870– December 1873
Millikan Stalker, farm superintendent	January 1, 1874– March 1, 1877 (?)
Sallie Stalker Smith, assistant secretary to Board of Trustees and Farm House matron	January 1, 1874– March 1, 1876
Mrs. Ellen (Ella) Milligan, Farm House matron *Note*: Sons Harry and William boarded at the Farm House while attending college.	March 1, 1876– March 1, 1879
Budd family: Joseph Lancaster Budd, acting farm superintendent, professor of horticulture and forestry; wife, Sarah Breed Budd; children, Etta May and Allen Joseph	March 1877– November 1877
John C. Hiatt, farm superintendent; and wife, Esther Macy Hiatt	March 1, 1879– March 1, 1880
Knapp family: Seaman Asahel Knapp, professor of experimental agriculture in 1880 and president of the college 1883–84; wife, Maria; and children, Seaman Arthur, Minnie, Bradford, Herman, and Helen Louise *Note:* Herman remained at the Farm House after the rest of his family left and brought his bride to live at the Farm House.	March 1, 1880– December 1885
Knapp family: Herman Knapp, professor of agriculture; and wife, Mary W. McDonald Knapp	December 1885– May or June 1887

Barrows family: Allen Campbell Barrows, professor of   May 1887–
    English literature and history; wife, Laura, and   December 1890
    children   (west half of
                     Farm House)

Loren Pease Smith, professor of agriculture and   December 1887–
    farm superintendent   November 1890
                     (East half of
                     Farm House)

C. P. Gillette, entomologist, experiment station   November and
                     December 1890

G. E. Patrick, chemist, experiment station   November and
                     December 1890

Wilson family: James "Tama Jim" Wilson, director of   January 1891–
    experiment station and dean of agriculture;   March 1897
    wife, Esther Wilbur Wilson; children, Flora,
    James, Peter, and Jasper
        Note: Esther Wilbur Wilson died at the Farm
        House on August 3, 1892.

Curtiss family: Charles Franklin Curtiss, manager of   summer 1897–
    experiment station, director of agricultural   July 20, 1947
    experiment station, dean of agriculture, dean
    emeritus; wife, Olive; and children, Edith, Ruth,
    and Helen, born in the Farm House on September
    14, 1901
        Note: Olive died in 1943; Charles died on
        July 20, 1947.

Vina Elethe Clark, librarian   1900–?

John Alexander Craig, professor of animal husbandry   1900–?

Elmina Wilson, instructor at the college and sister of   1900–?
    Olive Curtiss

Phyllis Curtiss Perry, student and niece of   1926 and
    Charles Curtiss   1929/1930

Elizabeth Hoyt, professor of economics and   1936–
    home management   spring 1948

Jean Packer, student   summer 1936

Elizabeth Curtis Willis, faculty member   September–December 1944

Frances (Mary Agnes) Carlin, professor of home economics   December 1947–
                                                                 spring 1948

Beulah McBride, assistant food manager,   December 1947–
    Memorial Union   spring 1948

Home management house residents: fall 1948–
    Instructor, Marquita Irland; students, Pearl (Peg) Ford,   spring 1949
    Kathryn Crowell Knapp,Patricia Howell Hutchins,
    Mary Lueder Nye, Pat McKee, Anita Ohlsen,
    Irene Morrison Phillips, Marion DeBois Nelson,
    Mary Alice Reinhardt, and Frances Craig; infants,
    Maria (Marcia Ann) and Steven Craig Curtiss

Andre family: Floyd Andre, dean of agriculture;   August 1949–
    wife, Hazel Beck Andre; children, Jacqueline,   July 1970
    Alice, and Richard
        Note: Hazel died in April 1956.

Marjorie Campbell Fountain, student and housekeeper   1957–1959
    for Andre family

Ellen Dihlmann, student and housekeeper for   1959
    Andre family

Norma Refle, student and housekeeper   1960–October 1962
    for Andre family

Dee Meadows, student and housekeeper   November 1962–
    for Andre family   May 1964

Appendix C
Residents of the Farm House, Alphabetical Listing

Residents	Dates
Andre, Alice	August 1949 to September 1959
Andre, Floyd	August 1949 to July 1970
Andre, Mrs. Hazel	August 1949 to April 1956
Andre, Jacqueline	August 1949 to September 1956
Andre, Richard	August 1949 to 1966
Backsen, Mrs. Alice Andre	August 1949 to September 1959
Barrows, Allan Campbell	March 1887 to December 1890
Barrows, Laura, and children (names unknown)	May 1887 to December 1890
Budd, Allen Joseph	March 1877 to November 1877
Budd, Etta May	March 1877 to November 1877
Budd, Joseph Lancester	March 1877 to November 1877
Budd, Sarah Breed	March 1877 to November 1877
Carlin, Frances (Mary Agnes)	December 1947 to May 1948
Christensen, Andrew	1869–1870
Christensen, Peter	1869–1870
Clark, Vina Elethe	1900–?
Craig, Frances	February–May 1949
Craig, John Alexander	1900–?
Curtiss, Charles Franklin	summer 1897 to July 30, 1947
Curtiss, Edith	summer 1897 to April 1919
Curtiss, Helen (born at the Farm House)	September 14, 1901 to 1922
Curtiss, Olive Wilson	summer 1897 to 1943
Curtiss, Ruth	summer 1897 to 1916
Dihlmann, Ellen	1959 school year
Dudley, Winifred	September through November 1868 and spring 1869 (?)
Emery, Sarah	1862
Fitchpatrick, John	March 1861 to March 1863
Fitchpatrick, Joseph A.	March 1861 to June 1861
Fitchpatrick, Liza	March 1861 to March 1863
Fitchpatrick, Martha	March 1861 to March 1863
Fitchpatrick, Mary	March 1861 to March 1863
Fitchpatrick, Nancy	March 1861 to March 1863
Fitchpatrick, Sarah	March 1861 to March 1863

Fitchpatrick, Sarah Hagy	March 1861 to March 1863
Fitchpatrick, William	March 1861 to June 1861
Fitchpatrick, William H.	March 1861 to March 1863
Foote, A. E.	October 1868 to 1870
Ford, Pearl (Peg)	fall 1948
Fountain, Marjorie Campbell	1957–1959
Gillette, C. P.	November and December 1890
Gilmore, Eliza	April 11, 1868 to August 1870
Gilmore, George	April 11, 1868 to August 1870
Gilmore, James	April 11, 1868 to August 1870
Gilmore, Jamie	April 11, 1868 to August 1870
Gilmore, John	April 11, 1868 to August 1870
Gilmore, Robert	April 11, 1868 to August 1870
Graves, Andrew Jackson	March 1, 1864 to April 10, 1868
Graves, Edward (born at the Farm House)	July 27, 1864 to April 10, 1868
Graves, Mary M. Meredity	March 1, 1864 to April 10, 1868
Hiatt, Esther Macy	March 1, 1879 to March 1, 1880
Hiatt, John C.	March 1, 1879 to March 1, 1880
Hoyt, Elizabeth	1936 to May 1948
Hutchins, Patricia Howell	1948
Irland, Marquita	September 1948 to May 1949
Knapp, Bradford	March 1, 1880 to December 1885
Knapp, Helen Louise	March 1, 1880 to December 1885 and again in 1900–?
Knapp, Herman	March 1, 1880 to May or June 1887
Knapp, Kathryn Crowell	spring 1949
Knapp, Maria	March 1, 1880 to December 1885
Knapp, Mary W. McDonald	December 1885 to May or June 1887
Knapp, Minnie	March 1, 1880 to December 1885
Knapp, Seaman Arthur	March 1, 1880 to December 1885
Knapp, Seaman Asahel	March 1, 1880 to December 1885
Lewis, Mary	1870
Mathews, Augusta	1869–1870
Mayo, Minnie Knapp	March 1, 1880 to December 1885
McBride, Beulah	December 1947 to May 1948
McCarey, Robert	1870
McKee, Pat	fall 1948
Meadows, Dee	November 1962 to May 1964
Milligan, Ellen (Ella)	March 1, 1876 to March 1, 1879
Milligan, Harry	March 1, 1876 to March 1, 1879(?)
Milligan, William	March 1, 1876 to March 1, 1879(?)
Nelson, Marion DeBois	fall 1948
Nye, Mary Lueder	fall 1948
Ohlsen, Anita	fall 1948
Packer, Jean	summer 1936
Patrick, G. E.	November and December 1890

Perry, Phyllis Curtiss	1926 and 1929–30
Phillips, Irene Morrison	fall 1948
Radford, John	1870
Refle, Norma	1960–October 1962
Reinhardt, Mary Alice Anderson	fall 1948
Roberts, Isaac Phillips	August 1870 to December 1873
Roberts, Margaret Jane Marr (and unnamed children)	August 1870 to December 1873
Robinson, Moses W.	March 1, 1864 to November or December 1866
Schmeal, Jacqueline Andre	August 1949 to September 1956
Smith, Loren Pease	December 1887 to November 1890
Smith, Mrs. Sallie Stalker	January 1, 1874 to March 1, 1876
Stalker, Millikan	January 1, 1874 to March 1, 1877
Stark, Charles	1870
Stark, M. (?)	1870
Stark, Nicholas	1870
Stark, Nicholas, Sr.	1870
Thomson, Hugh M.	January 24, 1867 to September 30, 1869
Townshend, Norton	October 1868 to 1869
Welch, Adonijah	September–October 1868 and spring 1869
Welch, Genevieve	September through November 1868 and spring, 1869
Welch, Harry	September–November 1868 and spring 1869
Welch, Mary B. Dudley	September through November 1868 and Spring, 1869
Welch, William	September–November 1868 and spring 1869
Whittacker, Helen Curtiss (born at the Farm House)	September 14, 1901 to 1922
Williams, Lizzie	1870
Willis, Elizabeth Curtis	September through December 1944
Wilson, Elmina	1900–?
Wilson, Esther Wilbur	January 1891 to death on August 3, 1892
Wilson, Flora	fall 1891 to April 1897
Wilson, James "Tama Jim"	January 1891 to March 1897
Wilson, James W.	January 1891 to April 1897
Wilson, Jasper	January 1891 to April 1897
Wilson, Peter	January 1891 to November 1891

Appendix D
Chronology of the Farm House

1846   Iowa is admitted to union as twenty-ninth state.

1858   Iowa Governor Lowe signs bill into law establishing a State Agricultural College and Model Farm.

1859   Trustees of college purchase 640 acres of land in Story County.

1860   Trustees Suel Foster, Daniel McCarthy, and E. G. Day select site for farmer's house and barns. Work begins on house in the spring. Trustees appoint Richard Gaines farm agent.

1861   Redbrick, 16-by-24-foot house with basement, kitchen, stairway, and two upstairs bedrooms is completed. A wooden washroom, 24 feet by 24 feet, is attached to north side of the kitchen. William Fitchpatrick and family sign two-year contract on March 1 as tenant farmers. Work begins on main 32-by-42-foot section of house. Civil War begins.

1862   On September 11 Iowa legislature accepts provisions of Morrill Act, establishing land-grant colleges.

1863   Board of Trustees appoints Peter Melendy as superintendent of college farm. Fitchpatrick and his family move to their own farm in March.

1864   Andrew J. Graves is appointed farm manager and moves his family into Farm House. Mary Graves gives birth to son Edward on July 27 at Farm House. Graves finishes plastering interior of house. State of Iowa awards lands acquired under Morrill Act to Iowa Agricultural College and Model Farm. Work begins on main college building.

1865   Civil War ends in April. Graves builds front porch that extends width of Farm House. A second wooden room, 18 feet by 30 feet, is added to east side of 1860 wooden addition for use by farm laborers. Brick privy is built to north of house.

1866   Graves installs two skylights above kitchen ell in second-floor hallway and north bedroom. In main section of house, he removes false ceiling in a small bedroom on second floor and wall between adjacent room to create one L-shaped room.

1867   Graves leaves farm. Hugh Muir Thomson becomes farm superintendent. James Gilmore becomes farm manager and also moves his family into Farm House. Ames now has 500 residents.

1868   Main college building is completed. Preparatory classes are held in the fall. College president-elect Adonijah S. Welch and his family move into Farm House.

1869   Official opening of college takes place on March 17. Isaac P. Roberts becomes superintendent of college farm and secretary of Board of Trustees. Male students report to Farm House for daily fieldwork assignments. Female students work in laundry, kitchen, and library.

1871   Roberts converts two east rooms of first floor into office and reporting room. Old office on west side of house is refurbished as parlor. Roberts moves bookcases, with 2,000 volumes, to first-floor east rooms.

1873   There are now three faculty houses on campus, plus Farm House. Faculty has seventeen members and there are 273 students on campus. Roberts resigns and Millikan Stalker becomes superintendent of college farm and instructor in agriculture.

1878   H. C. Hiatt serves as superintendent of college farm for one year. First telephone is installed at college.

1879   Seaman A. Knapp becomes superintendent and professor of agriculture and moves his family into Farm House.

1883   Seaman A. Knapp becomes second president of college. He lives at Farm House until 1885, when he resigns and moves to Louisiana.

1886   Herman Knapp, son of Seaman, takes over as head of agriculture. Two-room frame structure is attached to northeast back of Farm House, making it a duplex. Herman Knapp and his wife, Mary, share the house for one year with family of Professor Allen C. Burrows.

1887   L. P. Smith becomes superintendent and professor of agriculture and lives in east half of Farm House. Allen C. Burrows continues to live in west side of house.

1890   Steam-powered motor line, the Dinky, begins daily trips between Ames and college. Its tracks run just north of Farm House. Electric lights are installed on Onondaga (now Main) Street in Ames. In December, Allen Burrows moves away.

1891   James "Tama Jim" Wilson is appointed director of experiment station and professor of agriculture and moves his family into Farm House. He is given full use of house. Morrill Hall is built at a cost of $35,000. College enrollment is 425.

1892   Wilson converts first floor northeast room into a kitchen and west kitchen becomes a bedroom. His wife, Esther, dies on August 4. Her funeral is held in parlor of Farm House.

1896   Three water closets (bathrooms) are added to house and brick privy is torn down. Wilson has a furnace installed, connecting it to steam radiators.

1897   Wilson accepts appointment as U.S. secretary of agriculture and moves to Washington, D.C. Charles Curtiss accepts position as professor of agriculture and acting director of experiment station and moves his family into Farm House. The 1865 wooden room on northwest corner of house is torn down. Other nonspecific "extensive repairs" are made to house. House is painted white to protect bricks.

1898   New, smaller porch replaces original 1865 front porch. Electricity is extended to house. Interior floors and woodwork are painted. New wallpaper is applied to first-floor walls. Official name of college is changed to Iowa State College of Agriculture and Mechanic Arts, or ISC.

1900   North section of Main Building is destroyed by fire. ISC president's residence, the Knoll, is completed.

1901   Helen Curtiss is born in southeast bedroom of Farm House. Queen Victoria dies. Wireless telegraph comes to Ames.

1902   ISC president William M. Beardshear dies at Knoll. South section of Main Building is destroyed by fire. ISC enrollment is now 1,254. Charles F. Curtiss becomes dean of agriculture, a position he holds until 1932.

1907   Alumni Hall is completed and Charles F. Curtiss receives his Doctor of Science degree from Michigan State College.

1909–12   Farm House is connected to central steam system of college. Screened porch is added to west side of house with French doors leading into parlor. Exterior of house is stuccoed. Golden oak flooring is installed above original flooring in most rooms of house. Fireplace is added to west parlor and another to first-floor southeast room used by Curtiss as a library.

1926   Single-car garage is attached to north side of house and stuccoed to match rest of house. (Garage is demolished in 1970s.) Closets are added to third-floor rooms. Repairs are made to east kitchen.

1947   Charles F. Curtiss dies at Farm House on July 30, after living in house for fifty years. Edith had died in 1943. After Charles Curtiss's death, three women occupy house: Beulah McBride, Elizabeth Hoyt, and Frances Carlin.

1948   Interior of house is renovated and decorated for women of Department of Home Management. They live here for one year while caring for at least one orphan and keeping house as part of their college program.

1949   New dean of agriculture, Floyd Andre, and family move into Farm House. House is updated with new carpets, wallpaper, and paint. Andre lives at Farm House until 1971.

1965   Farm House named National Historic Landmark.

1971   Floyd Andre moves from Farm House and it stands vacant.

1972–76   College president W. Robert Parks appoints committee to assist with restoration of house. Interior is renovated with new plaster walls, paint, wallpaper, wiring, and plumbing. New shake-shingle roof is completed. House opens as museum on July 4, 1976.

1998–99   Exterior of house is renovated. Disintegrating 1912 stucco is removed, revealing crumbling brick and loose mortar. Brickwork is repaired. West porch is demolished and rebuilt. South porch is rebuilt. House receives new coat of stucco, copper gutters, and new roof on main house. Ramp-sidewalk is installed on west side of house, providing access to front porch entry.

2002   Using original gate from 1925 north arbor designed by Helen Curtiss, Iowa State graduating class of 2002 commissions reconstruction of arbor and gate as a class project (U2002.34). It is fabricated of Osage orange and Eastern red cedar wood. Today, a grape vine once again covers arbor.

2006   Fireplace that was removed from southeast first-floor room in 1948 is partially restored.

Sources

Address delivered at the Opening of the Iowa State Agricultural College, March 17, 1869. Gazette Premium Book Company and Job Printing Establishment, Davenport, Iowa.

Allen, William G. *A History of Story County, Iowa.* Iowa Printing Company, Des Moines, March 1887.

"Alumnus of Iowa State, The." March 1936 and March 1933. Alumni Association, Iowa State College, Ames, Iowa.

Ames Heritage Association. *Faces of Our Founders: The Early Leaders of Ames, Iowa.* Ames, Iowa, 1991.

Ames Intelligencer, Souvenir Edition, midwinter 1897.

Anderson, Marvin A.; Mahlstede, John P.; and Thompson, Louis M. Memorial Resolution for Floyd Andre. Iowa State University, Ames, Iowa, February 24, 1972.

Andre, Hazel Beck. "My Last Wonderful Days." *New Horizons,* fall 1956.

Andreas, Alfred Theodore. *Illustrated Historical Atlas of the State of Iowa, 1875.* Andreas Atlas Co., Chicago.

Annals of Iowa, 1863, Vol. 1. Reprinted by State Historical Society of Iowa with historial introduction by William J. Petersen, 1964.

Aurora (Iowa Agricultural College student newspaper), 1879–1892. Special Collections, Iowa State University Parks Library, Ames, Iowa.

Badger, Lewis. Diary of Lewis Badger, August 28, 1858, through July 1859. Unpublished materials. Courtesy of Charles Conger and Sandy Teig.

Bailey, Joseph Cannon. *American Education: Seaman A. Knapp, Schoolmaster of American Agriculture.* Arno Press and the *New York Times,* 1971.

Birth and Death Registry, Story County, 1892–1901. Story County Courthouse, Nevada, Iowa.

BOMB, The (Iowa State College yearbook). 1894: Representative Printing, Nevada, Iowa. 1895: Republican Printing Co., Printers and Binders, Cedar Rapids, Iowa. 1899 and 1900: Kenyon Press, Des Moines, Iowa. 1904, 1907, 1908, 1909, 1910: George A. Miller and Company, Des Moines, Iowa.

Carlin, Frances. Unpublished personal records. Call number 12/6/51, Box 1, Special Collections, Iowa State University Parks Library, Ames, Iowa.

Cemetery listings of the University Cemetery, 1880–1975. Facilities Planning and Management Department, Iowa State University, Ames, Iowa.

Christensen, Dr. Thomas P. *The Story of Iowa: A Children's History.* Holst Printing Company, Cedar Falls, Iowa, 1928.

Class of '97, Iowa State College. *Reminiscences of Iowa Agricultural College.* George A. Miller, Printing and Publishing Co., Des Moines, Iowa, 1897.

Curtiss, C. F., Guardianship petition for. File 8127, Story County Courthouse, Nevada, Iowa, September 24, 1947.

Dahlgren, Ronald J. "The Farmhouse." *The Iowan,* spring 1980.

Davidson, J. R. "Then and Now: Iowa Agricultural College, Past and Present." The *BOMB,* Republican Printing Company, Printers and Binders, Cedar Rapids, Iowa, 1895.

Day, H. Summerfield. *The Iowa State University Campus and Its Buildings, 1859–1979.* Iowa State University, Ames, Iowa, 1980.

Death notice of A. C. Barrows. *The* (Hudson, Ohio) *Independent,* February 14, 1908.

Death notice of Mrs. Esther Wilson. *Ames Intelligencer,* August 4, 1892.

Eppright, Dr. Ercel. *Century of Home Economics.* Iowa State University Press, Ames, Iowa, 1971.

First Edition. Special 90th anniversary edition, published by 1st National Bank, Ames, Iowa, spring 1993.

Fitchpatrick, William Jr. Diary of William Fitchpatrick, Jr., 1861–1864. Unpublished materials. Courtesy of Mrs. Phillip Allen, Nevada, Iowa.

Galland, Dr. Isaac. *Galland's Iowa Emigrant, Containing a Map and General Descriptions of Iowa Territory, 1840.* Printed by Wm. C. Jones, Chillicothe; reprinted by the State Historical Society of Iowa, 1957.

General Catalogue of the Officers and Students of Adelbert College of Western Reserve University, 1826–1895. Press of J. B. Savage, Cleveland, Ohio.

General Index of Deeds, 1856–1860. Book F, pp. 94, 95, 113; Book BVP, pp. 390–391; Book E, p. 102; Story County Courthouse, Nevada, Iowa.

Gerber, John C. *Pictorial History of the University of Iowa.* University of Iowa Press, Iowa City, 1988.

Goodspeed's Biographical and Historical Memories of Story County, Iowa. Goodspeed Publishing Company, Chicago, Illinois, 1890.

Gossard, Blanche. "People's Forum." Letter to the editor. *Ames Tribune,* October 4, 1939.

Hilton, Robert T. *Profiles of Iowa State University History,* 2d ed. Iowa State Information Services, Ames, Iowa, 1977.

Hilton, Robert. *Iowa State University Education for Pioneers and Pioneers in Education.* Iowa State University Information Services, Ames, Iowa, 1965.

Historical Sketch of the Iowa State College of Agriculture and Mechanic Arts, An. Published for the semi-centennial celebration, June 6–9, 1920, Ames, Iowa.

History of Jasper County, Iowa. Western Historical Company, Chicago, Illinois, 1878.

Honing, W. L. "James Wilson as Secretary of Agriculture, 1897–1913." Ph.D.

dissertation, University of Michigan, Ann Arbor, Michigan, 1964.

Hoyt, Elizabeth. Unpublished personal papers and memorabilia. Call number 13/9/51, Box 1, Folders 1–7; Box 2, Folders 21–27, Special Collections, Iowa State University Parks Library, Ames, Iowa.

In Memoriam, Edgar Williams Stanton, 1850–1920. The CLIO Press, Iowa City, 1920–21.

Index Record of Births, Summit County, Ohio. October 21, 1870, p. 29.

Iowa: Its History and Its Foremost Citizens, Vol. 2. S. J. Clarke Publishing Company, Chicago and Des Moines, 1918.

Iowa Agriculturalist, Vol. 9, No. 3, November 1908.

Iowa State Almanac and Statistical Register, a Facsimile Reproduction, Slightly Enlarged, of an 1860 Almanac. Supplement of the *Palimpsest,* January 1963. (Originally published by House of Luse, Lane and Company.)

Iowa State College Bulletin, College Directory. Vol. 41, No. 33, January 13, 1943, p. 30; winter quarter, February 1, 1948, pp. 28, 48, 59; fall quarter, November 1, 1948, pp. 27, 51, 64; fall quarter, October 25, 1947, pp. 221, 242, 254.

Iowa State College of Agriculture and Mechanic Arts Official Publication, College Directory. Winter quarter, Vol. 35, No. 35, January 27, 1937. Special Collections, Iowa State University Parks Library, Ames, Iowa.

Kehlenbeck, Dorothy. "Chronology of Important Events of the First 100 Years," 2d Preliminary Edition. Iowa State College Library, Ames, Iowa, November 1, 1957.

Knapp, Mrs. Mary McDonald. Diary of Mary McDonald Knapp, 1929. Unpublished materials. Courtesy of Mary Jean Knapp.

Lawrence, Roger L. "A Study of the Leadership of Seaman A. Knapp." Unpublished term paper. Farm House Museum Files, University Museums, Iowa State University, Ames, Iowa, 1953.

Lea, Albert M. *The Book That Gave Iowa Its Name.* State Historical Society of Iowa, Iowa City, 1935.

Life of Black Hawk. State Historical Society of Iowa, Iowa City, 1932 (reprint of 1834 original).

Mahan, Bruce E. "University of Iowa." *Palimpsest,* Vol. 52, No. 2, February 1971.

Meade, Gladys. *At the Skunk and the Squaw.* Greenwood Printing Co., Ames, Iowa, 1955.

Minutes of the Board of Trustees, Iowa Agricultural College and Farm, March 1865–1897. Microfilm. Special Collections, Iowa State University Parks Library, Ames, Iowa.

Morain, Tom. "Iowa, A Character Study." Presentation at the Brunnier Art Museum, Ames, Iowa, March 8, 1994.

Morrill Act. An Act donating Public Lands to the Several States and Territories Which May Provide Colleges for the Benefit of Agriculture and Mechanic Arts. 37th Cong., 2d sess., United States Statutes at Large, vol. 12, pp. 503ff, July 2, 1862.

Newhall, J. B. *A Glimpse of Iowa in 1846; or the Emigrant's Guide, and State Directory; With a Description of the New Purchase: embracing much Practical Advice and Useful Information to the Intending Emigrants, also The New State Constitution,* 2d Ed. W. D. Skillman Publisher, Burlington, Iowa, 1846.

Newton, Isaac. "Report of the Commissioner of Agriculture, Department of Agriculture, Washington, D.C., November 27, 1865," in *U.S. Agriculture Department Yearbook, 1865.* Reprinted 1972 with an article by Mrs. Max Molleston, Ames, Iowa.

"90th Anniversary of ISC, March 22, 1948." Special Collections, Iowa State University Parks Library, Ames, Iowa.

"One Man's Work." Curtiss Testimonial dinner at the Memorial Union, Iowa State College, Ames, Iowa, June 10, 1934.

Palimpsest, Vol. 52, No 2. February 1971.

Pammel, Louis Herman. *Prominent Men I Have Met.* Ames, Iowa, 1926.

Payne, W. O. *History of Story County Iowa: A Record of Settlement, Organization, Progess and Achievement,* Vol. 2. The S. J. Clarke Publishing Company, Chicago, 1911.

P.E.O. 1893 membership list, Chapter A.A., Ames, Iowa. Courtesy of Chapter A.A. P.E.O., historian Virginia Stafford.

Pohlman, Lynette. "Restoration Process, The Study of the Farm House." Master's thesis, Iowa State University, 1976.

Quinn, Kenneth. "Ninety Years of Accomplishment, 1947." *Iowa Agriculturalist* Vol. 46, No. 8, March 1948.

Registry of Deaths. Page W6, 93, August 3, 1892. Story County Courthouse, Nevada, Iowa.

Report of Secretary of Iowa State Agricultural College and Farm. 1859–1869, Book C, Acc. 340082, Special Collections, Iowa State University Parks Library, Ames, Iowa.

Resolution Concerning Dr. Charles Franklin Curtiss. Staff of Agricultural College, Iowa State College, Ames, Iowa, September 16, 1947.

Riley, Kathy M. "Life in the Farmhouse (on the ISU campus)." Unpublished article for Family Environment Special Problems Class, Series 4/8/4, Box 6, Farm House General Folder, Special Collections, Iowa State University Parks Library, Ames, Iowa, March 21, 1973.

Road Book A. Pages 86, 87, Story County Courthouse, Nevada, Iowa, 1853–1869.

Roberts, Isaac Phillips, *Autobiography of a Farm Boy.* Vail-Ballou Press, Inc., Binghamton, N.Y., 1916. Reissued 1946.

Robinson, M. W.; Thompson, H. M.; and Gilmore, James G. *College Farm Journal,* July 11, 1866, to March 17, 1870. Unpublished material. Special Collections, Iowa State University Parks Library, Ames, Iowa.

Ross, Earle D. *A History of the Iowa State College of Agriculture and Mechanic Arts, 1942.* Iowa State College Press, Ames, Iowa, 1942.

Ross, Earle D. *The Land-Grant Idea at Iowa State College, A Centennial Trial Balance, 1858–1958.* Iowa State College Press, Ames, Iowa, 1959.

Russell, J. S. "Young Man with a Yen for Serving Agriculture." *Des Moines Register,* Iowa Farm and Home Supplement, Section H, June 5, 1949.

Schmeal, Jacqueline Andre. "Farm House Memory." *The Iowan,* spring 1980.

Shank, Wesley. *Studies of Historic Iowa Architecture, Iowa State Univerisity Farm House.* Engineering Research Institute Project 101, Special Collections, Iowa State University Parks Library, Ames, Iowa, 1972.

Story County, Iowa, Census, 1885. Microfilm.

Students' Farm Journal. Edited by Agriculture and Horticulture Association of Iowa Agricultural College, Special Collections, Iowa State University Parks Library, Ames, Iowa, March 1887.

Studies in Iowa History, 1970. Iowa: The Home For Immigrants. State Historical Society of Iowa, Iowa City, January 1970.

Summit County, Ohio, Census. August 22, 1850, p. 446; June 19, 1860, p. 261; and July 9, 1870, p. 277.

Surveyor's Record Book A. Pp. 159, 241, Story County Courthouse, Nevada, Iowa, 1859 and 1867.

U.S. Census records, 1850, 1860, 1870, 1885, 1900. Microfilm, Ames Public Library, Ames, Iowa.

U.S. Survey Map, Township No. 83N, Range No. 241. Page 48, Story County Courthouse, Nevada, Iowa, 1867.

Waite, Frederick Clayton. *Western Reserve University: The Hudson Era.* Western Reserve University Press, Cleveland, Ohio, 1943.

Welch, Mary B. *Mrs. Welch's Cookbook.* Mills & Company, Des Moines, Iowa, 1884.

Williams, Martha E. "A Geographical Survey of the College Farm 1859–1869." Unpublished paper for Class Geography 490y, Series 4/8/4, Box 6, Farm House General Folder, Special Collections, Iowa State University Parks Library, Ames, Iowa, May 12, 1972.

Wilson, James "Tama Jim". Unpublished biographical materials, letters, collections of scrapbooks of news articles. Box 1, Folders 1, 10, 14, 18, 19; Box 3, Folders 3, 4; Box 4, Folders 1, 2; Box 5, Folders 1, 2, 6, 7; Box 8, Folders 5, 6, 7, 8, 9, 10; Box 9, Folder 9; Box 10, Scrapbooks 1, 2, 3; Box 11, Scrapbooks 5, 6, 7; Box 12, Scrapbooks 8, 9, 10, Special Collections, Iowa State University Parks Library, Ames, Iowa.

Wright, Luella Margaret. *Peter Melendy: The Mind and the Soil.* State Historical Society of Iowa, Iowa City, 1943.

Interviews
with Mary Atherly

Mrs. Phillip Allen, Nevada, Iowa, November 6, 1989.

Avis Lovell Andre, Ames, Iowa, 1992 and 1993.

Jacqueline Andre at the Farm House, June 1991.

Marie Beale, September 27, 1989.

Mrs. Edward Hardy, Jr., at the Farm House, August 7, 1989.

Jan Korslund, Ames, Iowa, July 14, 1993.

Isabel Matterson, Ames, Iowa, October 14, 1992.

Phil McCray, assistant archivist, Cornell University, Rare Books and Manu-
scripts Collections, University Library, Ithaca, New York, June 18, 1993.

Dean Nelson, Registrar's Office, Iowa State University, June 8, 1993.

Mrs. Jean Packer, Ames, Iowa, May 17, 1990.

Jeanette Rex, Ames, Iowa, October 2, 1989.

J. C. "Shorty" Schilletter, Ames, Iowa, July 12, 1993.

Theresa Taylor, Archives on Women and Medicine, Medical College of Pennsylvania, Philadelphia, Pennsylvania, June 11, 1993.

with L. M. Pammel

Ed Graves, June 14, 1922, notes in Farm House Museum files.

with Lynette Pohlman

Josephine Hungerford Dodds, October 31, 1974, notes in Farm House Museum files.

Polly Gibbs, November 4, 1974, notes in Farm House Museum files.

Bernice Graves, November 5, 1974.

with Neva Petersen

Sarah Fitchpatrick McElyea, ca. 1933, notes in Farm House Museum files.

Correspondence

Letter from Mrs. Avis (Floyd) Andre, Ames, Iowa, to Mary Atherly, July 14,
1993.

Letters from William M. Barrows, Hudson, Ohio, to Mary Atherly, July and
August 1992.

Letter from Hans J. Brosig, director Jasper County Museum, to Mary
Atherly, June 4, 1993.

Letters from James F. Caccamo, archivist, The Hudson Library and Historical
Society, Hudson, Ohio, to Mary Atherly, Nov.–Dec. 1992.

Letter from Rowene Clark, Genealogical Society of Wapello County, Ottumwa, Iowa, to Mary Atherly, May 27, 1993.

Letter from Charles Curtiss to President Stanton dated August 1902, Special
Collections, President Stanton files, Iowa State University Parks Library,
Ames, Iowa (copy in files of Farm House Museum).

Letters and correspondence between Carl Hamilton and members of the
Iowa State University physical plant during the restoration process, and
letters and memoranda to Restoration Committee members. (Copies in
files of Farm House Museum.)

Letter from Shirley L. Drewry, Newark, New Jersey, to Mary Atherly, December 19, 1992.

Letter from H. H. Kildee, dean of agriculture, to Mrs. Wallace Whittaker, October 13, 1947 (copy in files of Farm House Museum).

Letter from Mrs. Kathryn Crowell Knapp, Rockwell City, Iowa, to Mary Atherly, December 12, 1992.

Letter from Mr. Arthur G. Leonard to Bill O. (?), with notation "Helen from Bill O. to me to you Bud," August 4, 1947. (In file of Farm House Museum.)

Letters from Mrs. Marion DeBois Nelson, Oak Ridge, Tennessee, to Mary Atherly, 1992–1993.

Letter from Bob and Barbara Novak, Sterling, Virginia, to Mary Atherly, June 25, 1992.

Letter from Mrs. Mary Lueder Nye, Lincoln, Nebraska, to Mary Atherly, January 18, 1993.

Letter from Mrs. Janet Page to Floyd Andre, September 18, 1965.

Letter from Jacqueline Andre Schmeal, to Mary Atherly, July 18, 1990.

Letter from Gretchen Budd Smith, Ames, Iowa, to Mary Atherly, April 1992.

Letter from Mrs. Virginia Stafford, Ames, Iowa, to Mary Atherly, February 2, 1991.

Letter from Elizabeth Curtis Willis (Mrs. Ben), to Mary Atherly, July 25, 1990.

Additional Sources Used for Second Edition

Gradwohl, David M. "Archaeological Investigations at the Farm House: Progress Report," 1991. Unpublished report, University Museums, Iowa State University.

Nepstad-Thornberry, Tina N. "Phase 1 Archaeological Investigations of the Farm House Museum (13SR22) Iowa State University, Section 4, T83N-R24W, City of Ames, Story County, Iowa," 1999. Unpublished report, University Museums, Iowa State University.

Osborn, Nancy. "The Farm House (13SR122)." *The Society for Historical Archaeology Newsletter* 25.1 (March 1992): 26–27.

Prosser, Daniel J. "Architectural Assessment, Farm House Museum, Iowa State University, Ames, Iowa," September 25, 1992. Unpublished report, University Museums, Iowa State University.

Shank, Wesley. "Report on Proposal for Reconstruction for Library Fireplace," 2006. Unpublished report, University Museums, Iowa State University.

Weaver, Martin, of Martin Weaver Conservation Consultant, Inc. "A Conservation Study on the Farm House Museum, Iowa State University, Ames, Iowa," April 1997. Unpublished report, University Museums, Iowa State University.

Index